The Crofter Quine

by

Betty Fotheringham

Published by Betty Fotheringham

ISBN: - 13: 978 – 1478313625

10: 1478313625

To

Alfie

CONTENTS

(or far tae find athing)

Introduction

Chapter 1 – Fa's fa an fit's fit.   1

Chapter 2 – Settlin in an keepin oot o' langer.   6

Chapter 3 – Singsongs an spleuchans.   11

Chapter 4 – So school it was.   15

Chapter 5 – The war, gasmasks an beasties in ma hair.   22

Chapter 6 – Bounty an bombs.   27

Chapter 7 – Dad gets his dream.   30

Chapter 8 – Nosyin inta athing.   35

Chapter 9 – School during the day an peat fires at nicht.   40

Chapter 10 – Coos an cars.   44

Chapter 11 – Turkeys, jeuks an Christmas a get the go by.   48

Chapter 12 – Makin dae.   53

Chapter 13 – Tam - couthie cratur or coorse?   63

Chapter 14 – Neeps, tatties an the hairst.   67

Chapter 15 – Sausage sizzles an porkers.   73

Chapter 16 – Peace at last an catchin up wi the femily.   78

Chapter 17 – My world collapses.   84

Chapter 18 – Watter inside an oot.   87

Chapter 19 – Fae horse tae tractor.   90

Chapter 20 – Gettin oot an aboot mair.   93

Chapter 21 – Things tak a turn for the worse again. 96

Chapter 22 – Fae gallus quine tae Miss Smith.   100

Chapter 23 – Yefurup?   107

Chapter 24 – Ma courtin days are here.   111

And finally – About my birth mother.   116

Glossary   120

INTRODUCTION

Some authors claim that their fictional characters come to life and take over their book. The Crofter Quine started as a collection of stories about the lives of the Smith family seventy years ago, and these stories then took over and seemed determined to become a book. The tale starts in the early 1930's at a time when Wullie Smith was gaen up in the world fae cottar to crofter. Told through the voice of the youngest in the family, Betty, it brings to life the lighter side of the crofting world and many of the customs of the time. Much of the story is told in the couthy Mearns dialect as the author, usually called the "gallus quine" by her Dad, pokes gentle fun at him an some o' his wyes. A swear word appears now and again but these were rarely regarded as such by the family and certainly never caused offence. It is hoped this book will raise a smile or two and if this be so the author will be content.

Chapter One
Fa's fa an fit's fit.

One of my first memories was when I was three years old and sitting outside our home on the doorstep. I was a tubby little figure, often described by my Dad "As ready tae row's rin". A dark complexioned man passed by on the road some yards away. As he glanced in my direction, I lifted my skirt and showed him my knickers. As soon as I had done it I knew that I had sealed my fate and would definitely now come to a bad end. Even at that early age I understood that showing off my underwear to passing strangers was unacceptable and my conscience gave me such a hard time that day that I've been very careful never to do it again. As for the "bad end" bit, well at the time that seemed a long way off - so no worries there for a whilie. Anyway I had heard all about the bad end bit before. Every time we met someone we didn't know, my Mum would whisper to them and I would catch words like," She'll come tae a bad end that ane, bad blood will oot". The tone of voice was more worrying than the actual words which I didn't understand anyway, and ach there were mair interesting things tae think aboot.

This was a time in the early 1930's and we were living in "The Tin Kirkie", near Drumlithie in Kincardineshire, Scotland. This tiny building had been a kirk with monthly services at one time, but my memory of it was that it wisnae a very comfortable place tae bide in. It had a corrugated iron roof making it very noisy in heavy rain and it would have been worse in a winter hailstorm had we stayed there that long. It was a stopover for us until something better turned up.

My family comprised Mum and Dad, four brothers and a sister. Sandy was nearest to me in age but still ten years older, then came Gladys, eleven years my senior. Alfie was next and he was fee'd just up the road at Thrieplands and lived in the chaumer there. Alfie said they were nae mair comfortable tae bide in than kirks. After Alfie came Adam (always called Teddy) and then there was Wullie. They too would have been working not too far away because before the Second World War, people didn't usually travel far to find work. Teddy preferred sawmill work to farming although he still bothied. I do remember it being very cramped in the Kirkie, but we were about to go up in the world and live in a proper house. Our Dad, up to that time, had always worked as a farm servant. This was by any standard a very poor existence. Wages were tiny, made up for in a small part by the occupation of a tied cottage with a garden to grow vegetables and fruit, and there would also have been a supply of tatties, milk and oatmeal from the farmer. Farm servants were fee'd for six months at a time. If they didn't like the fee they were in, they went to the next feeing market, which took place twice a year, usually in the nearest market town and here they would hope to find a farmer who would offer them a job for another six months. They trusted that the new job, house and conditions of service would be an improvement on the last. I doubt that this trust was always justified. Farmers weren't necessarily good bosses and when a good one was found a cottar would bide a whilie, so there were few vacancies at the best farms.

My father was now ready to leave this life behind and move on as we say nowadays. He had found himself a job as a woodcutter and we were about to flit to a rented house at Roadside of Catterline, a few miles south of Stonehaven.
On first sight I thought this new hoose very big and grand. It had four rooms in fact, a coal shed attached and an outside lavvie. We had really come up in the world. Upstairs one large bedroom was for the four boys, only all at home at weekends and the other bedroom was for my sister Gladys and me. Downstairs was the kitchen, which today might be called a living room, although there is no real comparison. In this kitchen we cooked on a range. This had a swey and cruik from which to hang a kettle or a pot over the fire, an oven on one side and a boiler to heat water on the other. When lit the whole range was very hot and cooking could be done just by setting pans anywhere on the top and food would simmer away merrily for hours. It was an excellent method of cooking large meals for

big families, but it did have some drawbacks. Because the fire always had to be lit for hot water and cooking, the house got very hot in the summer. Another downside to it was the elbow grease, black lead and emery paper needed to keep it shining. Ours didn't shine often. There was plenty of hard work for my mother without that. In this room too we ate and washed up in a basin on the table. Mum and Dad also slept here in a box bed built into the alcove under the stair. At one time some of these box beds had two doors or curtains that closed them off during the day. We weren't grand enough for that. I envied my parents this bed in winter as this was the only room with heating, and I shared a bed with Gladys and Gladys didn't like me much. It was probably a sister thing for we each got along fine with our brothers.

The fourth room in the house was the best room. This was an unbelievable waste of space but it was the custom, and we had never had a best room before. It was furnished as a bed sit with a double bed, cheap second hand three piece suite in brown rexine and a wardrobe. This room was never used except when the minister came to visit, or there was a family crisis and a private space was needed. Fortunately neither ordeal happened often. The family's best clothes were kept in the wardrobe here, all reeking of mothballs, along with a pair of men's pyjamas. The PJs were for anyone in the family who needed a doctor's visit or who, heaven forbid, had to go to hospital. I did sometimes wonder how I was going to fare if I were ever ill for I slept in my breeks and liberty bodice, and I knew the family pyjamas were never going to fit me. Luckily we never needed doctors, they had to be paid, and since most health problems are self -righting anyway, we either ignored them or self treated. Aspirin was much used for headaches, but we didn't think to use it for any other pain. A dab of iodine soon sorted out open wounds. Regularity called for castor oil or sometimes I had syrup of figs. Lucky me! Sore throats were dealt with by fastening one of Dad's sweaty socks round the neck at bedtime, held in place by a safety pin. If my throat ever bothered me I kept very quiet about it. My father's sweaty socks were something you didn't want to get up close to. For a cold we had a toddy before going to bed and this helped us to "sweat it out". Even I at the age of four was given this poison of whisky, honey and boiling water. I loathed it then, and today I still can't stand the smell of whisky, but perhaps it had some merit, for it certainly knocked us out, or would that maybe have been the sweaty sock?

The kitchen range gave us hot water for washing hands and faces and the men for shaving. All this was done in the kitchen with no privacy, but it gave a friendly relaxed atmosphere with much joking and laughing. For instance Teddy always teased Dad about being bald. When Dad washed his face he washed his head as well, quite vigorously, with droplets of water flying in all directions, much as a spuggie does in a birdbath. Teddy would laughingly tell him that he wisnae sae much bald, but jist hid an awfu wide pairtin. Even at his age Teddy's own hair was already going thin and Dad would retaliate with "Jist you wait an we'll see fa'll hae the last lauch in a few years' time".

The wooden coalhouse with an earthen floor doubled as a washhouse with a boiler, wooden tub and washboard for all the clothes washing. Yes, the laundry was done in the coalshed. We thocht nothing o't and Monday was always washing day. Dad and the loons would bring their dirty clothes home on a Saturday afternoon and go off on Sunday night with their clean things. Sometimes there wid be good naiturred argiements aboot fit sark belanged tae fa, but at the end o't a, they each hid a clean sark, semmit and socks for the next week and peace reigned. I don't remember dungarees ever being washed and with all the resin from working with trees, these trousers were so stiff they could almost stand upright on their own. Jackets too, mostly made of Harris Tweed were never cleaned.

All our water came from a well a couple of hundred yards up the road. It was carried down to the house in metal pails and even when empty these pails were quite heavy. This was woman's work and I had to help too, takin the skin aff ma shins many a time with the sharp edge on the bottom of my half full pail. No wonder we didn't waste water. Later when I was a little bigger, I tried having baths in the coal/washhouse and for this Mum described me as being "different". "Can ye nae be like ither fowk?" she would say angrily. Being like ither fowk meant washing mostly jist the bits ye could see and having a rub down all over now and again. Mum was always telling me I was different and I would come to a bad end. She did seem tae hae a richt illwill at me at times, bit it wis jist her wye and it didna bother me much at that age.

The laundry of course was my mother's job. After a scrub on the washing board in the wooden tub, which was backbreaking work, the clothes would then go into the boiler where the water would bubble away until they were clean. Rinsing came next, then through the mangle and outside to dry. It was an exhausting Monday for my mother and the main meal that day would be something made from Sunday's leftovers. This was usually stovies. I loved them then and still do. Most of today's stovies are a poor imitation of that dish of long ago, or is that my memory I wonder?

Mum would take some gravy (leaving in a little of the fat for flavour) and any chopped up meat left over from the Sunday pot roast and add chopped onions, diced potatoes and Burdall's Gravy Salt with perhaps a scrap of extra water. Long slow cooking followed until the potatoes had broken down and needed very little mashing. The stovies were fairly dry, light brown from the gravy salt and eaten with a fork accompanied by a cup of milk and homemade oatcakes. There was always plenty to go round and they tasted superb.

Chapter Two
Settlin in an keepin oot o' langer.

Every day of the week would have its different task for my mother. After the washing would come the ironing, done of course on the table, protected from the heat by an old blanket. A triangular shaped heater would be taken red hot from the fire (it had a hole for the poker to fit into) and placed inside a box iron. Down came a shutter and once the sole had heated up it was ready for use. A second heater would go into the fire in readiness as a replacement. Mum did sometimes use a flat iron as well.

There was a baking day when oatcakes, scones and pancakes would be made on the girdle. Little baking or cooking was done in the oven, as controlling the temperature was very much a hit or miss affair. Anyway the oven was usually full of kindling drying out for lighting the fire in the morning. Then there would be a house cleaning day and one weekday was left over for odd jobs and shopping. We were lucky to have a general shop right next door to us. Our milk came from a small croft a few hundred yards further along the road. Fetching this in a little metal pail with a lid was my job. I would follow this very elderly man into his dairy and watch while he filled our pail, all the while keeping an eye on the dreep at the end o' his nose. I was convinced that one day it would fall into our milk. This never happened, but it was nearies at times.

Our large garden was very productive. Using farm dung for fertiliser and growing crops in rotation, we were self sufficient in fruit and vegetables for much of the year. The tatties were pitted, ingans plaited and hung in the shed, and the carrots were stored in boxes buried in sand. Brussels sprouts stood proud all winter, even in the snow, waiting to be picked for the weekend meals, jist so's I could get a row for nae likin them. Nowadays still a big treat for me is to politely decline sprouts at any meal, jist because I can! The garden was Dad's domain, helped out by any of my brothers who happened to be at hand. We had plenty of fruit for jam making. The taste of a home made scone hot off the girdle, with fresh farm butter (not made by the dreepy nosed crofter by the way) and Mum's jam, will live with me forever. And yet we still craved shop bought cakes at times. Mum used tae say "You eens dinna ken fan yir weel aff".

We kept hens to supply us with eggs, and occasionally we would spare a bird for the pot. Keeping hens was a very natural thing to do, for they only needed a hoosie at night, and either a ree in a part of the garden, or at certain times of the year they could roam freely. They were mostly fed on kitchen waste. All food scraps from the table went straight to the hens' pail, and all vegetable peelings would be boiled up and go to them as well, so they actually cost very little to feed. They did need a few handfuls of corn (oats) every day but that didn't cost much, and in order to get eggs with strong shells the hens needed a constant supply of grit. This could be bought, but supplying it was my job. Any old china cups, saucers or plates were broken down into tiny chips either with a hammer or small stone and left out for the hens to help themselves. I am told it was the lime in the china that the hens needed for their eggshells. We kept one cockerel. He bossed the hens around and would strut about thinking he was God's gift to every hen around him, which I suppose he was in a way. His presence meant that when we had a clockin hen, and provided he had done a bit more than strut his stuff, we would eventually get a few baby chickens. These little balls of fluff would, when grown, boost the numbers, and since we only ever needed one big chief, any young cockerels would be for the pot.

I don't remember up to that time ever having any expensive toys, but I always had a pair of wooden stilts made by my Dad. I had made friends with the boy next door whose parents had the shop and the two of us made good use of empty Lyle's Golden Syrup tins. We punched holes in both sides just under the rim and threaded a loop of string through each of them. The lids then went firmly back on, and with a tin under each foot, we would pull the strings very taut with our hands and just about manage to clump around on our new toy. I don't know if these tins had any advantage over the stilts, but perhaps we liked them because we had made them ourselves. I do know they were very noisy and we fell off a lot, but bairns were easily pleased.

Everyone had a gird, nae cleeks though, jist a stick tae ca an auld bicycle wheel roond and roond wi, but that did us fine. For indoors, I had a creepin Jesus and this was made using an old wooden cotton reel with v-shapes cut round both ends to give it grip, elastic, a piece of wax candle, a tack and a spent match.   Once assembled I would wind up the elastic with the match, then let go and hope that it would creep along the linoleum slightly faster than a snail. It was as exciting as watching paint dry and yet I still treasured it.

Of course I played with marbles, even making my own. A few yards from the house a road roller driven by steam would park for a few nights when doing road repairs near at hand, and I would place rough balls of clay inside its big open wheels. When the roller returned the following night I would retrieve my bools, now perfectly shaped after trundling round and round all day.   These "marbles" were fairly fragile and were easily smashed by a glass one or a steely, but making them was fun. The few children I came in contact with before I started school were no better off than I was and I certainly didn't feel deprived in any way by the lack of shop bought toys.   Perhaps I envied my friend Stanley a little because, as his parents owned the shop, he always had plenty of sweets. Still I was really glad to have him to play with because, being part of an already grown up family, did mean that I was lonely much of the time. However something very strange was about to happen, and I was to get a shop bought toy that dreams were made of.

One day a black car drew up at the door. This was an exciting event because our Dad had only just gone from pushbike to motorbike and he was very proud of this steppie up in life. (He drove hunched over the handlebars of this bike, flat cap clamped firmly back to front on his head, and travelling only a little faster than when on his old pushbike, bit he wis a happy man.)

From the back of this unexpected car stepped a very beautiful lady. I didn't know much about film stars, except that Mum was often told at that time that I looked just like Jean Harlow, who apparently was a film star. This meant little to me because I was considered too young for the pictures, (it sounded good though to be likened to a film star), but this lady who had come to call was exactly what I imagined a film star to look like. She had a brief conversation with Mum, then I was told to fetch my coat and go in the car with this stranger. I was given no explanation. I didn't know who she was or what to call her. I didn't know where I was going or whether I would be coming back. I remember I went quietly enough, although very puzzled and a little scared.

We travelled a very long way that day and I was sick out of the window of the car. I don't think I had ever been in a car up until then, for we didn't know anyone rich enough to own one. When going on a bus Mum would sit me on a newspaper telling me that this would prevent me from being sick. It usually worked, but the newspaper had been forgotten that day. I would have been unlikely to have reminded anyone, for I found it very embarrassing trottin for a bus ahint my mither wi a newspaper under my oxter, as if I winted tae tell the hale world that I wis likely to be sick.

We arrived at a small croft and were met by a man, woman and small boy. The man wasn't too welcoming I felt, the lady certainly was, and the boy I was very curious about. I remember thinking he looked a bit like me. I did find the courage to ask who he was, but got no answer to my question. So fit wis new aboot that? I have no recollection now of how I spent that day, but I was taken home again in the evening. As this nameless lady was leaving, she took from the boot of the car a small pram and a teddy bear. These were gifts for me. Nothing as wonderful as this had ever happened to me in my short life, and I was so proud of my treasures. That teddy was to become a much loved bear.

As soon as the lady had gone I was full of questions for my mother. Who was she? Where did she take me? Why this wonderful present, for it wisna even my birthday? I was given no answers or explanations and Mum seemed quite badtempered about the whole business, telling me as usual that bairns should be seen and not heard. The evening of that exciting, but scary day, I hid under the kitchen table as I often did. The chenille cover reached all the way to the floor on all sides, and I found this a wonderful place to hide. If I had been in trouble, I would hope to escape punishment by diving out of sight in there and like that evening, I could listen in to the grown ups' conversation and pray they would forget I was there. I was often discussed when we had visitors, and so it was on this occasion, but to my great disappointment I didn't understand any of it.

Chapter Three
Singsongs an spleuchans

I loved the weekends at Catterline when everyone was at home. Dad and my brothers were quite gifted musically. Dad played the melodeon and sang a little. The singing bit wasn't always encouraged because I only ever heard him sing one song, and that was "The Star o' Rabbie Burns". It has many verses and it was generally considered fortunate that he couldn't remember them all. The others played the harmonica or "mouthie", piano accordion or "the box", and Teddy's favourite was the chanter. He had great ambitions to graduate to the bagpipes, but got little encouragement from any of us on that one. Pipe bands at a great distance can be quite stirring, but a learner piper skirlin awa in a hoose wis mair than a buddy could stan. Mum and Gladys were onlookers and listeners at the musical evenings, and I was generally considered to be tone deaf. Reluctantly I admit to this being true, but in my next life I plan to be a singer. Meanwhile I was fobbed off with a comb covered wi thin paper which you put to your lips and blew through, and it fair made yer lips dirl I can tell you. Alfie had a beautiful tenor voice. We were all very proud of him. He did have a record made at one point in his life, and after auditioning for the BBC when the war was over, we would all have loved for him to have followed a singing career, but it wasn't his dream so it didn't happen. I doubt that he ever really regretted it, finding in later years no lack of opportunity to entertain audiences with his singing.

These family evenings usually ended with sharing the latest bars. (These were jokes of a suggestive nature.) This would be the signal for Dad to get out his pipe. He was a heavy smoker, an we didna mind his fags so much because most men smoked, but more than those, Dad loved his pipe and his Bogie Roll tobacco. For us pipe reek in an unventilated room of an evening was hard to bear. Depending on the direction of the wind there would often be blow backs of reek from the lum, which were dealt with by stuffing it with newspaper when the fire was unlit, and setting fire to this to burn away the build up of soot. If the blowbacks wirna too bad a handfu o' saut was thrown on the flames tae bring doon the soot. But on a windy night wi smoke from the fire, our Dad would light up his pipe, our eyes wid rin and we wid hoast an sneeze. (No doubt we put it on a bit.) Dad would just laugh, nothing would stop him enjoying a draw. The whole experience was really a ritual to him and today, if smoking wasn't proven to be so unhealthy, I'm sure some stress therapist would be advocating it as an excellent form of meditation.

It wid start wi the pipe comin oot o' a singed pooch, having frequently been stuffed awa afore the last of the embers were out. This object of our disgust would then be firmly tapped a few times as near the fire as Dad could be bothered stretching, emptying the old ash from the bowl. Fortunately our Mum wasn't house-proud. Then out came his pocketknife and the bowl of the pipe would be carefully scraped to give it a final clean. That done, a sharp blow through from the other end would send stinking spit an dottle a ower the place and leave all of us now thoroughly disgusted. (Later he might cut himself a bit of cheese wi the same knife, hygiene also wasn't high on the list of priorities.) A box of matches would emerge from his pocket, usually Swan Vestas, no new fangled lighters for Dad and these would be placed beside the pipe in readiness. Next, out came the spleuchan, a round tin affair. When given a squeeze in just the right place the lid would fly open revealing the object of our loathing – the twists of Bogie Roll. After this came the paring of shreds of tobacco with his knife and the very careful filling of the bowl of the pipe. The success of the lighting depended on the skill of filling, so it was worth takin time ower and no conversation would take place while this ritual was going on. Finally a match would be struck and offered to the pipe accompanied by a lang seuch on the mouth end. If it lit first time the look of concentration on Dad's face would change to one of peace and joy, and once more he wis for speakin to again.

Clouds of smoke would rise around him while we all coughed and spluttered, again making much more of our discomfort than was the actual case. My brothers would have a dig at him "Can ye nae at least get a new spleuchan Dad, that ane stinks". Now they didn't expect him to heed their pleas, but lo and behold one Saturday night, when they had gone off to Stoney to do whatever young men do on a Saturday night, Dad went to the pictures on his own. Mum an I aye bade at hame because I was still considered too young for the pictures. While in the town Dad decided that he would surprise us all, and he bought a new spleuchan from the tobacconist, but then felt so nostalgic aboot the auld ane that he couldna bear jist tae throw it awa. He placed it on a window sill near the bus station, in the hope that someone would come along and take a fancy to it, and treat it with the same reverence and loving tender care that he had given it for the whole of his smoking life. He duly arrived home and proudly showed Mum and me his new purchase.

Well you don't need a university degree to guess what happened next. Off a later bus came my brothers, and in the door they burst laughing and jostling each other like the overgrown schoolboys which they undoubtedly were. Dad's old spleuchan was produced and presented to him amid much laughter. They were thinking he would now have two spleuchans for them to complain about. But the laugh was on them when Dad produced his brand new pouch, quite modern looking compared to the metal box thing. It wasn't long though before he had his Bogie Roll neatly tucked into the old box, there was nae mair speak o' new spleuchans an from that night on we a jist tholed his reek in silence.

P.S. to the saga o' the pipe.

Now, kept in Dad's pocket along with his beloved pipe, was always a handful of granny sookers. As a special treat I would be given one from time to time. Granny sookers as we all know are usually white, but these were always a light to dark brown colour, depending on how long they had shared a bed wi the pipe. I would complain bitterly about the state of them to Dad, but all I ever got from him wi a lauch was "Ach, sook it clean quine, a little bittie dirt niver hurt onybody". An him being my Dad, of course I believed him.

Chapter Four
So school it was.

Just after we had settled into our grand big hoose, the headmistress from Catterline School stopped by and asked how old I was. The age for starting school was five but on being told I was only four, she announced "Well, she's big enough, so she's old enough". So school for me it was.

To get there I had to use Shanks pony, i.e. walk, but I was very pleased about going. I was going to need new wellies and anything new at that time was very exciting as we didna dae new very often. Looking back it seemed a long way to school, about three miles, I guessed. Being only four years old, still short and dumpy with little legs didn't help, perhaps it even clouded my judgement over the actual distance. Quite recently I checked out the mileage and had to admit to my son that my memory had been a little inaccurate. On being pressed further about how far it actually was, I had to own up that it was probably not much over a mile. The younger generation I've noticed can be richt smug when they catch ye oot. Best of all though about starting school, and even better than the wellies, was that I expected to get a beautiful new leather schoolbag. I pictured this bag in my mind at night before I went to sleep, and it was the first thing I thought about in the morning, well that an ma new wellies. My brother Sandy was about to leave school just as I started. He would leave on his fourteenth birthday in March and I was to start the following Monday. In those days there were no recognised starting and leaving dates, or if there were this school didn't heed them.

As the big day got closer, I plucked up courage and asked my mother when we could shop for my new schoolbag, to be told, "Naa, naa, Sandy's aen'll dae ye fine, we canna waste money like that". Devastated I appealed to Dad when he came home for the weekend, but with no success. Mum was treasurer and Dad rarely went against her. I'm sure that from the day they married until she died, he would never have known how much money they had. There was a common acceptance between them that all money was handed over to her, and she decided how it was spent. First priority was Dad's Bogie Roll for his pipe and then his fags. After that we were all at her mercy. "Wants" weren't high on her list of priorities, as there were always so many "needs". I'm sure other families were just the same.

My disappointment over the schoolbag was great, but there was a God in heaven, as I was shortly to find out. My excitement at starting school was nothing compared to Sandy's at the prospect of leaving it, and that afternoon he arrived home in great delight. He was now fourteen. He had left school forever and had a job waiting for him as a butcher's boy in Stonehaven, starting on the Monday. What more could he wish for? Later that night Dad asked him to bring the schoolbag so that he could mend it ready for me on the Monday. Our Dad soled, heeled, patched and studded all our shoes and boots. During his time working on farms he had always worked with horses, so had taught himself to mend the leather harnesses. It was a small step further to mending shoes. Our Dad could do anything, or so I believed, and I didn't judge him for being roch an ready. That wis jist his wye.

At first Sandy was a bit taken aback to be asked for his schoolbag. Finally he reluctantly admitted to Dad that, in his excitement at leaving school, he had raced out of the building, down the road to a little bridge over a burn and had thrown bag and books over it into the water. As I said, there is a God in heaven after all and my dream of a new bag became my reality.

On that first day I set off for school greatly excited. Although not anything like the three miles, it was still a long walk for me with my short chubby legs, but I had my new schoolbag on my back and I was very proud of it. In my bag I had some milk in a bottle for playtime, and as the weather was still cold, I had a penny for soup, this was made at the school by the cleaner, and she must have had a limited choice of recipes. If it had been possible for me to have thrown a sickie, I would have chosen to do so on broth days. I had no chance of that though, only a high temperature or a broken bone would have got me out of going to school, we didnae dae "no weel" in oor hoose. Also in my bag I had a paper poke with a piece of bread and jam, and a Burdall's Gravy Salt tin containing a little cocoa powder mixed with sugar. The teacher supplied hot water to make a warm lunchtime drink

Sadly my excitement was to be short lived. Very short lived indeed. At the start of the first day it was discovered by the infant teacher that I was left handed. I was told to use my right hand, but I remember quite clearly repeating "Na, I winna". The headmistress was called through from her room to deal with me. I can still see her in my mind. Her hair (it was red), glasses, tweed suit in a sharny green colour, her blouse was the colour of my skin when I had jaundice, brown brogue shoes and thick ribbed stockings. This was a woman who showed no mercy. For nearly three weeks I was strapped daily by her, because I wouldn't change to using my right hand. I finally gave in, but being left cleekit, my writing was very poor and day in and day out, right through school, I was told "You can't write". Well, was it any wonder? I was not an isolated case this was standard treatment in many schools at that time. Today it would be serious abuse.

The strap or tag was a fearsome thing, and even when I wasn't on the receiving end, my stomach would churn when the teacher took it from her desk. It was about three inches wide with thongs at one end. This was the end that did all the damage, not only to the hand of a four-year-old, but up the arm too. It took courage to keep your hand outstretched, but pulling away would double the punishment and if the teacher caught her own leg as a result, the consequences were even worse. Some of the big brave lads considered the extra belting worth it. I admired them for that, but never shared their courage.

The tag was hard to thole and used daily for many reasons. For instance, a small burn ran by the road leading to the school, and if we were wearing our wellie boots, we would walk up this burn, but the teacher would examine our feet on dry days and wet boots meant one of the strap. What did the woman think wellies were for, I wonder?

Because sweets were only a very occasional treat (except for my new friend from the shoppie), on the way to school we would dip a wet finger into our cocoa and sugar mixture and lick it. This would almost always leave a telltale brown mark round our mouths and any stain would be another one of the belt. It must have been one of the few schools where you could have had two of the tag before your backside hit a chair. During lessons more than two spellings or sums wrong, and it was one of the strap for each extra wrong answer. For those who had difficulty learning, this meant that the swelling on their hands and wrists from one day wouldn't have subsided before the next, and the teacher would strap alternate hands each day. My anger towards the injustice of that headmistress is as strong today as it was then, and as a result of that unfortunate start, I hated school right through until I left on my fifteenth birthday. If there had been a brig an a burn handy that day, I ken far my bag an books wid've landed.

This wasn't my only problem on starting school. The whisperings that took place at home seemed to have spread to the other pupils. I could hear them talking about me. I even heard "Dinna play wi her. She's got bad blood". What was this mystery that surrounded me? Why just me, why were my questions never answered? It was lonely at home when the loons and Dad were all away, but I was fortunate to have the boy next door to play with, because he at least didn't seem to mind the whisperings. It was as if a shadow hung over me. I was part of a large family and yet, perhaps because Mum kept telling me I was different, at times I felt different. I felt I just didn't belong. Could it simply have been the big age gap between us?

Around this time my oldest brother Wullie got married and he and his wife Violet came to live with us. In a little while Violet gave birth to a baby girl. This baby was almost immediately taken ill, and died at only a few weeks old, just after being christened in the house and given the name Gladys after my sister. Violet barricaded the door of their room on the day of the funeral and it had to be broken down to allow little

Gladys to be buried. This was a very dark time for us. Later, all the loving care that Violet would have bestowed on her baby was transferred to me. She saw that I was clean and tidy for school and I felt loved and mothered. I was very sad when Wullie and Violet moved out to their own place. I was lonely again, but I still had the weekends to look forward to and Sandy brought another little bit of excitement into our lives.

He was a very keen cinemagoer and about that time the "Lassie" films were being shown. Our Sandy was also a dog lover and he set his heart on having a Shetland collie dog just like Lassie. He even gave his puppy this name and he idolised her. He hadn't long started working but it was becoming clear to him that he wasn't cut out to be a butcher. He was so pleased to get back home to Lassie in the evening after a boring day in the shop, when fowk wid torment him by comin in an askin for things like "hingin mince". Sandy was quiet and gentle with a lovely sense of humour, but he didn't appreciate the "hingin mince" jokes. Back at home he would play with and train Lassie night after night and at the weekends too He soon had her doing all sorts of tricks. Collie dogs' mouths are not the best for "carrying" but Sandy quite quickly had Lassie trained to pick up and carry things. His aim was to get her to go down the road to the shoppie and bring back the daily paper, and after a time she did this every day just fine. He was so proud of her and boasted about his dog to the other loons all the time. They did get a bit tired of him at times on the subject of Lassie.

One weekend the three of them had gone for a walk up the road with the dog in tow. Sandy as usual went on and on about how clever Lassie was at picking up things and carrying them. Teddy, now gye weary of Sandy's constant boastin aboot his dog, said, "Well, ye'd better be richt, for jist tae test ye I drappit ma wallet back doon the road a bittie an I hope tae God yon dog's picked it up, for I hivnae lookit roond". Of course, all heads turned, but there was Lassie with the wallet in her mouth and Sandy's heid wis mair swallen than iver. He had his dog trained to do tricks too, but one rebounded a bit on my mother one day, an she wisnae best pleased I can tell ye. I wis there an

I saw it a. On this day a stranger was standing down the road waiting for a bus. She was dressed in a very smart coat and had a dainty little hat perched on her head. I was playing at the door wi Lassie and no doubt had got her all excited. Lassie, almost fully grown and quite big by this time, saw the woman and bounded down the road. She leapt up from behind and deftly whipped the hat from her head, racing back with it to me and dropping it at my feet. All just as Sandy had trained her to do with his brothers' flat caps. Of course the lady screamed and then let out a torrent of abuse directed at the dog or me, I wasn't sure which. I ran off to hide under the table, leaving my poor mother who hadn't seen what happened, but who had come to the door to see what all the fuss was about, to sort it out. She sorted out Sandy too when he came home that night.

Sandy would also hide things and train Lassie to sniff them out. This again rebounded on him one Saturday night. After finishing work he met up with Teddy and Alfie to go to the pictures as was their usual on Saturdays, but at some point Sandy bought himself a box of chocolates and hid them in his raincoat. He had no intention of sharing them.

Arriving home off the last bus, he sneaked upstairs to the big bedroom he shared with the others and hid the chocolates in his bed under the blankets. These chocolates were for him later after everyone was asleep. Or that was his plan anyway. Clever Lassie though had other ideas, and did what Sandy had trained her to do. She sniffed out the chocolates, but instead of bringing them to him she ate the lot, leaving Sandy a very sticky bed that night. Not a word of sympathy did he get from anyone and it was a long time afore Teddy and Alfie let him live that one down.

Sandy left his unfulfilling career as a butcher's boy soon after that and started working in the sawmill and bothying with the others. I missed him because ours was then a house of women from Monday to Friday, but I had Lassie for company and she was much loved.

School dragged on and soon I was out of the infant

classes and into the big room. This was a bit like leaping out of the frying pan and into the fire for me. Because Catterline was a school with only two teachers I was now going to be taught by the strap mad headmistress. I learned pretty quickly how to avoid the belt for myself but I was always deeply upset and resentful when one particular boy, small for his age and needing a little more time perhaps than the rest of us to learn anything new, was belted every single day. I do feel that my resentment towards this teacher may have partly helped me in later years, to find the courage to fight in anyone's corner when I have seen an obvious injustice. I'm grateful for that.

I appeared to be reasonably clever at this school, although still being told I couldn't write. Classes were very small, so to be in the top three wasn't too difficult. With a different teacher I'm sure I would have enjoyed learning. One thing that stays clearly in my memory and always seemed unfair was when some of the older boys were sent out on a Friday afternoon to clean and wash the teacher's car, while the rest of us had to stay in the classroom and work. That could never happen today and nor should it.

Chapter Five
The war, gas masks an beasties in ma hair.

In 1939 when I was six, war was declared on Germany. Of course trouble had been brewing for some time and I could feel the tension in our house in the build up to this. Wullie was in a reserved occupation so did not do war service. Teddy was already in the Territorials so he was first to be called up. Shortly after, Alfie joined the Air Force and Sandy was just desperate to do the same but was too young. Teddy was still training down in England when a Bren gun carrier overturned on a hill and rolled over him breaking bones, and of course ending his service career before it had really begun. This was a huge disappointment to him and after a very long time recuperating he was discharged on health grounds on a meagre disability pension. I clearly remember the courage of my mother at the time of Teddy's accident. She had never been on a train, nor had she ever travelled more than fifty miles from where she was born, but with Alfie's girlfriend Cathie, she immediately packed and left for Barrow in Furness to be with Teddy.

Much later we were told that a fortnight after his accident, the remainder of Teddy's unit left for abroad and were in active combat. The whole unit was wiped out within the first few weeks of fighting, so injured though he was, Teddy was lucky to be alive. Although the whole family was affected by this news, my mother in particular was greatly distressed for the families of the soldiers in Teddy's regiment.

Alfie was sent to France almost immediately after training. There he only just escaped German capture by clinging on to the outside of a lorry for many miles to reach Dunkirk when France was overrun. From there he got one of the last places in a small boat back across the English Channel. He was then sent to Lerwick in the Shetlands, before going to Sierra Leone in West Africa where he was a dispatch rider. He also had a couple of spells in Arbroath and Glasgow.

Sandy finally managed to get into the Air Force by lying about his age. After training he celebrated, if you could call it that, his eighteenth birthday, on a troopship bound for India. From there he marched through Burma and on to Japan. The side of the war that Sandy saw was not nice and as with many others no doubt, he came home years later a changed person. Of course he had gone from boy to man but it wasn't just that and although I still found him gentle and kind, the sparkle and some of the fun side of him had gone.

Gladys was sent off to an ammunition factory in Coventry and our house was very quiet. At least Dad was working nearby now and was home every night. Mum worried about her loons as she called them all the time. Although she knew Teddy was now safe, there was always the question of how he was going to earn a living with his disability. Alfie and Sandy were a constant worry to her being so far away, and of course there was no home leave while they were abroad. Letters came irregularly and we had to rely on the radio, newspapers and the Pathe News at the cinema to get the bigger picture of the war. When any letter did arrive from any of my brothers, Mum was very excited and would wait for the sound of Dad's motor cycle in the evening. She would rush out clutching the letter in her hand to show him before he could even get off his bike.

My mother wouldn't hear any complaint from us of hardship at this time, always reminding us of what the people in the big cities were going through with incessant bombing. She said too that with growing our own vegetables, we didna ken fit food rationing wis. We had never grown flowers much but along with everyone else we turned all available space over to vegetable and fruit production. "There's naethin comin ower us" Mum would say. She was right, and truth to tell we had never had many luxuries in our house, so fit we niver hid we didna miss.

We had eggs from our hens and Dad would sometimes come home with a rabbit or hare for the pot. Mum cooked rabbit in a way that made it taste just like chicken. Another dish we had quite a lot during the war was hairy tatties. Dried salted pieces of cod were plentiful and these were boiled along with tatties and then mashed together. The tiny pieces of cod running through the potatoes looked like hairs, hence the name "hairy tatties". Served with our own vegetables it was no doubt a nutritious dish but could hardly have been called appetising. A didna look forrit tae hairy tatties nicht much.

We always had a frame on the side of the house, made by Dad of course. This frame had crossed slats of wood into which nails had been hammered through from the back. During the herring season, (in other areas of Scotland they used haddock), these were filleted, impaled on the nails and left in the sun to dry. Were they salted? I don't remember. After drying they were called speldings. Being so near the village of Catterline getting fresh fish too wasn't a problem, but mackerel, although much eaten today because of its healthy image, would have been a last resort. They were considered the scavengers of the sea, but I remember they were very plentiful and easy to catch even from the rocks.

Not long after the war started we were all issued with gas masks. Mum and I went separately on the back of Dad's motor bike down to the school to get ours. I found it difficult riding pillion behind Dad. He was quite stout, well very stout actually, an I couldna get ma erms roond him tae hang on. I thocht he hid a bit o' a cheek ca'in me as ready tae row's rin. When sharing his bike rides, I had two fistfuls of jacket, I dug my knees in on either side and prayed I wouldn't fall off on the corners. Apparently I always leant the wrong way when cornering, even when I was shouted at. It was not only difficult when riding pillion with Dad it was scary too. I do know that he had never taken a driving test because there wasn't such a thing until many years later, and I doubt that he would have had any actual driving instruction. On the other hand, as I said earlier, Dad never drove fast, nor did he overtake any other roaduser on wheels if he could avoid it.

The gasmasks came in square cardboard boxes, and we bought waterproof covers to keep them dry. They had to go everywhere with us at all times. We had a practice drill every morning at school, because we were told that seconds wasted in putting on this thing could cost us our lives. I can't remember how we were to know if a gas attack was imminent, but the general view was that it wasn't going to matter much anyway, for no one believed that our masks would protect us. These boxes wir a richt nuisance tae cairry aroon wi's a the time though.

With everyone's focus being on the war, the whisperings around me had stopped and I was having a much easier time at school with the other children. Instead we all had the evacuees to worry about and we stood united against this common enemy. I cannot tell you how ashamed I am of how I felt about these children at that time. Because of the heavy bombing children were taken from their homes in the big cities, and had to be taken in by anyone with a spare bedroom, living in any area regarded as relatively safe from bombing. It's difficult to imagine the heartbreak this caused for the children and their parents.

Not all those who gave these poor children a home did so willingly, so there was resentment all round. The evacuees who came to Catterline were from a very poor area of one of the big cities and they found it hard to fit in. Up until then and for some years on, we hadn't found it necessary to lock doors or put things away in sheds. Now milk from doorsteps in the village was vanishing and anything else lying around was taken. The people of the village had pilfering, sometimes serious, in their midst and more resentment built up over this.

These poor children just didn't fit in at school with the rest of us either. But worst of all, they brought impetigo and head lice with them. I was lucky and didn't get the former, but I certainly caught the beasties in my hair. My head was shaved, leaving only the long hair from the crown of my head to fall down and cover my baldness. What was left of my hair was washed with paraffin to kill the nits and after that I had a going over with a been kame. This was a nightly ritual. I felt dirty, ashamed, guilty and above all resentful, because this had happened to me. At school I didn't dare go near the evacuees in case their beasties loupit from their heids to mine, an it wid start a ower again. Unfortunately my mother's concern for the poor people in the big cities didn't extend to me catchin beasties fae them, and it was considered to be a ma ain fault. I felt very hard done by.

But think of these poor children. Whatever conditions they had been living in, it was still their home and they had been taken from it. They came to a scary world, often living with people who really didn't want them, and going to such a different school with children who resented them. Looking back I am right to feel ashamed, not perhaps so much now because of my behaviour, but of a world that could let this happen and believe it to be the right thing to do.

Chapter Six
Bounty an bombs.

Shortly after the start of the war Dad found himself a member of the Air Raid Patrol, ARP for short, which brought him the advantage of a much better gas mask. Perhaps this was why the rest of us didna think much o' oors. If oors were supposed to save oor lives fit did the ARPs need a better ane for? He did also get a steel hat and an armband, but that was it as far as a uniform went, and it didn't seem much to give a man to defend his country. I was never very sure what Dad was supposed to do and I'm not sure he did either. I imagined he went patrolling the countryside looking for spies. Through a child's eyes this made him a very important person indeed. I am sure the reality was more like him keeping an eye out for any house carelessly showing a light, but Dad did patrol the beach in case of an enemy landing. This was actually a very real threat in the North East of Scotland and strangers were viewed with great suspicion. We were suddenly very security conscious in that respect. All homes had to have the windows completely blacked out after dark. In our case this meant wooden frames covered in special black fabric. These were fitted over all the windows at night. A very thick curtain was hung inside the front door, and great care was taken when entering or leaving the house after dark not to let a chink of light show.

Although the war seemed a long way away, in reality this wasn't so. The passing merchant ships now hugged the coast for safety. They were escorted of course by Royal Navy vessels, but there were frequent attacks on them and we would watch these battles at sea from our front door, always making sure that not a scrap of light showed. It was very scary. Cargo from these damaged ships was washed ashore and eagerly collected after high tide but only after dark. This was always shared, with some of whatever it might be finding its way to the older folk, and with so many of our men away in the Forces, their wives and families were not forgotten. Of course it was illegal to do this as all bounty was the property of the Crown, but our King was a long way away living in a palace.

One incident I clearly remember was when a message went round for all able-bodied men to be on the beach this particular night. Small tubs of lard had come ashore and as soon as darkness fell they were collected from the beach and shared out, some being quietly left at the back doors of those who couldn't be expected to help. I think my father's motor bike must have come in handy on that occasion, but could it have been that *preventing* this sort of thing was part of his ARP duties? I would have thought so. This lard was such a welcome addition to our rations. We had never heard of calories, far less counting them. Cholesterol too was away into the future. All our food from the garden was healthy and organic. That's another word we hadn't heard of, for we didn't know any other way as we had no chemicals to speak of then. With this lard we enjoyed everything fried for a whilie. Skirlie, eggs and chips were my favourites. Mum made that tub of lard last a long time, an niver a bit o' herm did it dae us.

We quickly learnt to identify enemy planes by their engine noise. They mostly passed overhead at night, but in daytime we would run for cover if we heard a plane approach. We could easily tell the difference between a bomber going to find its target with a full load of bombs and one returning empty. The engines of the fighter planes were different again, and I was particularly frightened of them, but then they were the ones attacking our ships so close by, lighting up the sky at night with their gunfire.

One particular night I shall always remember. It was a Saturday. Dad had gone to the pictures, Mum was ironing and I was sitting in an armchair when it suddenly glided a little distance over the linoleum floor. "Mum, my cheer's movin" I said. "Dinna be daft, quine" she replied. She had hardly finished speaking when there was the most deafening din that seemed to go on and on, punctuated by explosions, it probably only lasted seconds. I shot off my chair and out of the door, into the porch which had a corrugated iron roof. The noise above was even worse here, so I opened the outside door and ran hell for leather up the road to a neighbour's house. I burst in through their unlocked door to find the family sheltering under the table. I squeezed in beside them.

My mother found me eventually, and after the noise died away, we all sat and marvelled that we were still alive. Now we had some idea what it was like to be bombed. A plane had, we guessed, been unable to find its target, and had to drop its load in order to have enough fuel to make it back home across the North Sea. We were unlucky to be the target, but oh so lucky to escape with our lives. Apparently I had been particularly so, because, when daylight came, we found the road I had run up in the dark was littered with bits of shrapnel and any one of these bits could have killed me. The flat roof of our porch was inches deep in earth, stones and more shrapnel. The only damage we suffered was to our coalhouse door. Not so lucky was our neighbour who supplied our milk. One of the bombs had landed in a field very close to his croft house, badly damaging it. The morning after the bombing, this poor man was found wandering around outside, completely disorientated and in total shock. He was taken to hospital and never returned to his croft.

Another of the bombs had exploded behind our house, which was why we had all the fall out around us, and a third landed in a field near the road I took to get to school. It didn't explode, so I had to make a long detour until the Army had time to come and set off a controlled explosion.

Word had reached Stonehaven of the bombing and Dad arrived back home on the next bus. This should have been his big chance to shine during the war and far wis he? Sittin in the picture hoose! Captain Mainwaring of Dad's Army couldn't have done it better!

Chapter Seven
Dad gets his dream.

A couple of years after the war started, Dad was felling a wood a few miles north of Stonehaven on the Netherley road, and each day he passed a tiny croft that was about to become vacant. After many years of working as a farm servant, it seemed he had always had a dream of being the farmer or crofter at least. Taking on even a croft was an enormous leap of faith for both Mum and Dad. Mum had very little education and apart from working in the various farmhouses, if this was part of Dad's contract, she had never had a job. Her father died when she was very young and she had to leave school to look after her siblings. This allowed her mother to go out to work and support the family. There was no financial help or support of any kind in those days. She told me that later she did some sewing for a shop in Ellon as an outworker, but her skills in that direction were as roch an ready as Dad's were in the things he made, so I rather doubt if that story was true. But certainly Mum could count reasonably well, she would write as she spoke, but could never have filled in a form of any kind. She did read the Press and Journal, exasperating Dad greatly by telling him the latest news before he had a chance to read it for himself. The fact that she always got hud o' the wrang end o' the stick exasperated him even more. She would never read a book or even a magazine and I was not encouraged to either. Books were for men and women had no need of them, and because I longed for books this also showed how different I was, I was often told.

My Mum did have a wonderful quality though, she trusted and believed in Dad completely an wid hear naethin against him iver. So if he winted to be a crofter then she wid be a crofter's wife an that wis that.

I doubt that Dad's education was much better. His mother died young and there was always a veil drawn over his father so what secrets lay there we never knew. I ken femilies often have a secret or twa hidden awa, bit oors seemed tae hae mair than maist an some o' them hid tae dae wi me.

Dad, although his writing skills were only slightly better than our mother's were, was an avid reader. Mysteries and Westerns were begged or borrowed but they would never be bought. Despite Mum's ban or maybe because of it, I would sneak any of these I could get my hands on up to the bedroom, and read them under the bedclothes by torchlight. Mum was aye complainin aboot the flashie batteries nae lastin, an I aye hoped Gladys widnae tell on me. She had come back from the munitions after only a few weeks. From my hidey-hole under the table I heard that she wisnae cut oot for war work. There seemed to be a bit o' a mystery wi her an a, but it wis tae be a few years afore I understood aboot Gladys.

There were long discussions about taking on this croft. It was called Fishermyre, and it was three miles up the Netherley road going out of Stonehaven. After my innocent miscalculation of the mileage to Catterline School I had better say that it was just *under* three miles. The croft consisted of only a few arable fields and some heathland with boggy areas where nothing would grow. A little way down the road there were two tiny fields, on one of which stood the ruin of a house. This was called Betty's Croft (nothing tae dae wi me) and this too was part of Fishermyre. It was a gey run doon place but Dad wis a for takin it so a deal wis struck, hands were spat on and shaken. He hid his ain place at last and he wis a happy man.

What excitement I now had in my life. I would have these nearly three miles to go to school after the move, so I wid need a bike. Not a new one of course, that wid niver dae, but Dad did a deal on a second hand ane. This bike was long past its sell by date and had no brakes, but of all the bikes I had over the years, I don't ever remember having one that had. If a bike had wheels an hanlebars tae steer wi, fit mair wid I need? I could pit ma fit doon fin I winted tae slow doon or stop, an watch the sparks flee fae the tackets in my sheen. It wid've been richt fine tae hae sheen withoot tackets, jist tae see fit it wis like. Years later the first pair of shoes I bought for myself had rubber soles – jist so's Dad couldna pit tackets in them. I learned to ride my bike on the country road that ran past our house, falling off onto the grass verge for a soft landing until I got the hang of it. I felt really grown up an I wis gaun tae a school in a toon. I could hardly wait.

This move was a much bigger step up in the world than the one of moving into a rented house and to be worthy of this, Dad had got rid of the motor bike and bought a car. Now we could arrive at the croft in style. At that time farmers were always known by the name of their farm, so Dad would no longer be plain Wullie Smith, but would be referred to by his peers as "Fishermyre". Ye wid hae thocht he wis aboot tae be knighted by the King himsel. He wis awfu prood o' his new title.

I was bursting with excitement the day we moved. I was nearly nine an nosy. Everywhere I turned there was something to explore. The only farm I had visited regularly up to that time was near us at Catterline. It had Clydesdale horses a mile high wi backs on them that my short fat legs couldn't begin to straddle. My wee airms could barely reach the mane to hang on, yet it was always assumed that my greatest wish was to be thrown up on the back of one of these beasts for a ride. At that time too girls didn't wear trousers, so my knickers would be flashing as my skirt flew up. The boys would giggle at this and not only was I embarrassed, but remember I had sworn a lang time afore to gie up flashin my breeks in public. At Fishermyre there wisnae a horse in sight, I felt safe and since I wisnae needed for onything, I was free to explore.

This house too had four rooms with a milkhouse built on to one end, and if we had been posher we would have called it the dairy, but ca'in it a milkhoose wid dae us fine. There was a byre and a barn at the other end, and the house standing in between these other buildings, gave me the impression that it was more of a mansion than a house. Mum said I aye hid big ideas, as if that wis a crime. I was still going to have to share a bedroom wi Gladys but I suppose I couldna hae a'thing. Mum and Dad now had their own bedroom and that was probably the first time that had happened since their marriage. We had the usual kitchen and best room. We hid an ootside lavvie again that, with so much countryside around us, we avoided if at all possible. In the winter I sneaked in to the byre for a warm pee. The milkhouse had a stone floor for coolness with wide shelves on which stood the big, very shallow, metal basins for the milk. In these basins the milk would settle and the cream would rise to the top to be skimmed off for butter making. We had a wooden churn too which that day fascinated me, but which I later came to hate. The milkhouse was also equipped with a marble slab, butter clappers and a wooden stamp with "Fishermyre" deeply carved mirrorwise on it. This was for stamping our pats of butter when we came to sell them. All this equipment and much more about the place, had been bought with the usual spittin an handshakin from auld Pyper who, with his daughter Lizzie, had farmed the croft before us.

Narrower shelves higher up in the milkhouse would come to hold the cheeses Mum assured us she would make, and the presses for these were all there waiting. With a cow, rennet and butter muslin she would be ready to go. In spite of her lack of formal education Mum was very knowledgeable and skilled in all things around the croft. If an animal was ill she even knew which wild plant would treat it, successfully too in most cases. We only needed a vet for serious things.

This milkhouse was a whole new world to me and that day I loved it. It was only later that the reality of being a dairymaid wore a bit thin. Trying to get cream to separate into butter in a hand turned churn when there was thunder in the air, was exhausting work. I would arrive home from school to find my mother "Near awa tae a greasy spot", she would say, and it would be "You'll hae tae tak ower quine". After a day at school and a long bike home, I wid raither hae hid a skive ahint the straw soo wi ane o' Dad's books that I'd pinched, but butter churning it would have to be. I might have argued with my mother, but it wouldn't have done any good and she would only have told Dad and I never, ever went against him. It was assumed anyway that even at that age I was part of the croft and expected to do my bit along with Mum and Dad. I didn't feel hard done by. This was how it was on all crofts and small farms. Most of the time I liked the responsibility I was given, and only now and again did I complain.

Chapter Eight
Nosyin inta athing.

As I said, moving in day was exciting for me. There were various sheds around the croft to nosy into, all in a serious state of falling down. Apart from the stone buildings, everything about the place was falling down. The previous owner was well into his eighties and according to my Dad "He was bloody eeseless at biggin onything". That was condemnation indeed from a man as roch an ready as he wis. I had to acknowledge that although Dad's standards weren't very high, he did appear to have some.

We had also taken over some of the livestock with the croft, but that mostly amounted to a few scraggy hens and a cock to rule the roost. Mum said "Thon hens widna even mak a decent pot o' soup, far less gies eggs". There was an auld coo tae, but even in my dream world, I couldna see masel stampin many pats o' butter wi "Fishermyre" on them fae this coo.

The hens lived in what Dad dismissed as "scratchers". These had been made by propping up long lengths of brushwood to form a tepee shape. Dad called this brushwood "hag". He even made that sound derogatory. To a woodcutter hag wis only fit for burnin. Thinking about it now, the hens were probably quite happy in their scratchers. After all, their ancestors lived in trees. These tepees were dotted all over the place, and Dad was very embarrassed by the sight of them, and they would have to go and quickly. As "Fishermyre" he had a reputation to build.

Wandering around the croft I made all sorts of interesting finds. There was the usual midden that I kept well clear of, and there was the previous occupant's rubbish heap. Now it was a wonderful place to nosy into. Rubbish heaps on a croft weren't quite as you might imagine them to be. Absolutely every scrap of leftover food would go to the animals, so there was little or no smell from the heap, unlike the midden which wid've garr'd ye bowk. Anything that could be, would be recycled. Much of what was left a nosy bairn would view as treasure.

Bits of china with a pretty pattern on them for instance, would conjure up a picture in my mind of genteel ladies having afternoon tea in a cup with a saucer. We only ever had saucers when anyone came to visit. These ladies would have maids, who would serve cucumber sandwiches with the crusts cut off. I had never tasted cucumber or even knew what one looked like, but I must have heard them mentioned. Maybe the lady who looked like a film star who came to see me lived on cucumber sandwiches. Quite likely, I thought. I dreamed of her from time to time and wished she would come again.

Perhaps it was a scrap of pretty fabric that brought dreams of me owning a new dress. One that had never been worn by anyone else, that fitted me in all the right places, that I didn't have to grow into or have let down, and that had been bought in a really big, expensive shop in Aiberdeen. Oh, such imaginings from the rubbish heap! To be fair to Mum, we did have rationing with clothing coupons, but new anything was never high on her list of priorities. Of a hand me down dress she wid say "It fits far it touches an it'll dae ye fine". But I had my dreams.

It was quickly realised that the rubbish heap was piled above the spring that supplied all our drinking water, so we were very careful not to add any more rubbish to it. Dad thought it best not to try and clear the existing rubbish away, in case that released toxins into the water, but yet we were rarely ill, and the family pyjamas stayed in the big wardrobe unworn. I did get some of my own years later when I started working, and could pay for such luxuries myself, and it didn't do me any harm to sleep in my knickers and vest until then. At least I had grown out of the liberty bodice and into a semmit like everyone else.

Near the spring was a mill lade with a waterwheel. I had no idea what these were for, but I walked up the dry lade out of curiosity and found a very pretty dam. There was a wooden shutter between the dam and the lade with an old poker sticking through a hole. So what was a nosy bairn tae dae? After pulling out the poker to take a closer look at it, I had to step smartly to the side as the water gushed through and down the lade.

Seconds later there was enough force to set the waterwheel in motion. Terrified I threw the poker as far as I could into the middle of the dam and ran, shouting "It wisna me, it wisnae me".

The waterwheel turned a rod going into the barn and inside this barn, which I hadn't yet had time to explore, was a threshing mill. The turning of the rod started the mill working, and because of all the noise of me shouting and the clanking, squeaking and grinding of the mill, I was suddenly surrounded by Mum, Dad, Gladys and the removal men. In spite of all the carfuffle Dad was curious about how this contraption worked. Finding some sheaves of oats lying on the floor, he fed them into the mill and quite quickly it all came out at the other end, but with only one exit point there was straw, grain and chaff altogether in a heap on the floor. "It's a hamemade affair", said a disappointed Dad, followed by, "Bloody eeseless mannie". Looking back now, I think to make a threshing mill of any kind must have taken some doing, and loyal as I was, I don't think Dad could have done it.

But Dad wasn't angry with me, although he was a bit put out when I admitted that I'd thrown away the poker. Because this mill had no on/off switch, we had to put up with the noise and vibration of it until the dam ran dry. That was the first and last we saw of the mill and waterwheel working. The mill was a bit like the scratchers as far as Dad was concerned. It had to get the go by as soon as possible or he would never live it down. After all he was no longer a cottar, he had achieved his ambition, owning his own land, and he had his reputation to think of. It must have been a great day for him. As for me, well, cottar, woodcutter or farmer, my Dad would always be the greatest.

We soon settled into our new home but quickly discovered some of the drawbacks. One very serious problem was when, on the first night, Dad went past the midden as it was getting dark to see it heaving, and on closer inspection, he found the cause – rats, a lot of rats. Auld Pyper just hadn't been able to cope on the croft for some years, and maybe he just didn't realise how serious having so many rats about the place was. Mum and Dad worried about the hens at night, because Dad said the scratchers would give them little protection. The good healthy hens brought from Roadside had now joined the others, and we didn't want to lose any of them. Trying to rear chickens was out of the question until the rats had been dealt with, but there was no easy solution, and it was the possible diseases they might be carrying that was most worrying. Dad tried a few different ways of dealing with the rats, most of them I have forgotten. He solved the problem in the end in a very cruel way that you really don't want to know about. Overnight every rat left the croft and with the help of a few cats we didn't have a serious recurrence.

I was very happy having all these buildings and land to roam around in, and I made the most of it. Even in the early days I had chores, but to me it was all a great adventure. I suppose I felt it was unfair that Gladys didn't have regular chores as I had, but I was aware there was a mystery with her as well. Just before our second move up in the world Gladys had started using the surname Bisset. She was sometimes Smith and sometimes Bisset. She spent most of her time at home as her jobs didn't seem to last long. Either she didn't like the job or her employers didn't like her. She was also subject to quite violent outbursts of temper when it was best to keep out of the way. This was more easily done at the croft for I soon had lots of secret places I could disappear to. Apart from a serious incident one day when she pushed me to the top of the stairs and sent me hurtling down, I generally considered her a tiny thorn in my side. I felt sure all sisters must quarrel.

In retrospect I can see now that this was the start of her slight mental impairment. Perhaps Gladys had always had this and it was now getting more noticeable. Who can tell? This mental problem dogged her for many years until finally discovered and controlled and of course this was why she couldn't keep a job. As already explained we weren't a family for doctors, but I doubt that the medical profession could have helped her at that time.

I wandered through the nearby woods, where Dad had been working when he found Fishermyre, and I found places to return to again and again. I was now in a wonderful world studying the trees and the peat bogs where I found such a wealth of interesting plants. It was undoubtedly at this time that my lifelong love and interest in plants started. Maybe auld Pyper hadn't been much of a crofter latterly, but his daughter Lizzie had been a very keen gardener. We took over a garden full of every perennial plant imaginable. In summer the perfume and the colours of the flowers were wonderful. I loved it all but sadly growing food was the priority during the war and soon it all had to go.

Chapter Nine
School during the day an peat fires at nicht.

It was just such a pity that I had to start a new school, I was so content on the croft, but school was after all why I had got a brakeless bike and learned to ride it. I enrolled at Fetteresso Primary School and because we didn't change classes at Catterline in line with other schools, I fitted into neither one class nor the other. The headmaster decided to put me in the class above the one I had been in previously, and that, together with a class size three to four times bigger than I'd ever known, meant that I failed everything miserably, or that was how I perceived it to be. My troubles started with my handwriting being very bad and we all know why that was. The fact that I was naturally lefthanded was never at any time explained to this teacher nor to any subsequent one. It was pretty much downhill after that. I was very unhappy. Country children at that time were always rather looked down on, probably because some of us were shabbily dressed compared to the toonsers as we called the others. This wasn't the only reason though for me, the "bad blood will oot" and the "bad end stuff" all started up again. Lots of whispering went on around me, and I was now old enough to worry about it. Why was I always being told I was different? How did I have bad blood? And what did that mean anyway? I made no friends at Fetteresso School and my lowest point was when, because of possible air raids, all the country children were asked to stand at the front of the class. Those who lived in the town then had to choose one of us to take to their homes in the event of the siren being sounded and the school closed. The siren would sound when there were enemy aircraft in the vicinity and the possibility of an air raid. As I had already survived one of those, I was very frightened at the prospect of another. No one wanted to take me home and I stood there alone for what seemed like ages, until finally one girl took pity on me. The shame of that incident I never forgot.

However I was lucky too, there was a family of two boys and two girls living not far from Fishermyre, we became friends and I visited them as often as my chores allowed. We had a lot of fun together exploring the countryside round about. We particularly liked wandering around Ury House. This was a vacant mansion not far from us with beautiful trees and shrubs in the grounds. There my imagination would take wings, and I saw myself as a lady living a grand life in the big hoose. I not only had my own bed, but a whole bedroom to myself, with beautiful clothes to wear and elastic in all my knickers – not a safety pin anywhere. With brakes on my bike and books to read, what more could I want? Oh yes – shoes with no tackets.

Reality though had to take over from daydreaming, and I was about to be introduced to another chore. Along with the croft we had the right to cut peat in the moss just down the road from us. "We winna hae tae buy coal iver again" Mum said. One evening, the three of us set off on this new adventure. On arrival at the moss it was very difficult to find which part of this was ours. We had a map showing our "bit", but in reality we were standing in a large piece of heather covered ground with no reference points. The only signs of peat working were obviously many years old, so we couldn't really get a bearing anywhere. That didnae bother Dad for long. Finally he said "We'll jist pick a bit an start diggin".

Now the fact that no one else seemed to work their part of the moss should have told him something, but na, na we'll seen get the hang o't he assured us. Dad skimmed off the heather, really hard work, so that Mum and I could make a start cutting the peat. We had peat spades that most likely were acquired in the deal along with the scratchers. It was very heavy going. Dad wanted the peats to be neat, tidy and above all whole. I had a problem with all of those limitations, particularly the "whole" bit, because my peats always broke in two and no matter how carefully I placed them on the ground, you could see the join. My excuse was that I wis really ower little tae be cuttin peats. Soon I was relegated to the job of building them up in rickles to dry. These too had to be neat, tidy and in rows. I was gettin awfu tired o' worryin fit ither fowk thocht o's. For someone as roch an ready as Dad wis, he could be gie pernickety at times, especially when whatever we were doing could be seen from the road. Cuttin peats definitely wisnae for me.

On top of all that needed to be done on the croft, it was difficult at times to keep up with the peats. After school I was always the one sent off on my bike to turn them all so that they could dry out before they could be taken home and stacked. We had little idea how much we would need for fuel to last until the following year, but we stopped digging when Dad's enthusiasm ran out. Mum's and mine hid run oot a lang time afore that. It was jist possible we might need a coalman efter a, an maybe we hid discovered why we were the only anes cuttin peat.

The irony of it was that one of the first really big fires we built with the peat, set fire to the chimney. What a night that was. Afterwards Dad declared the lum hidnae been swept for years, an probably that wis the first decent fire the hoose hid iver seen. This was another black mark against poor auld Pyper. It was a serious fire though. We were three miles from town with no telephone and none near. To prevent the floor catching alight Dad was shovelling and barrowing red embers out of the kitchen as they came down the lum. Mum and I were running around outside making sure that the sparks coming from the top of the chimney didn't set anything alight in the yard. The car was sitting at the gate with the engine running ready to fetch the fire brigade, but even I knew if it came to that, the whole place would be alight afore the fire brigade got to us.

There was a fireplace in the bedroom I shared with Gladys, and Dad was just about to take a maill hemmer to the chimney there in the hope that he could pour water in and quench the flames, when there were signs that the fire was dying down. After all the clearing up was done Mum and Dad stayed up all night, in case any sparks were still smouldering around the croft that might be fanned into flames. We had a very narrow escape from disaster that night, and I doubt that auld Pyper's lugs hid stopped dirlin for days wi fit Dad ca'ed him. I'm quite certain the peats had nothing at all to do with the chimney fire. This was a disaster waiting to happen, but maybe that night sounded the death knell o' the peats, for I heard Mum say later "Fae noo on we'll jist burn sticks an coal like abody else". This meant instead o' turnin peats every nicht, I could spend mair time sittin daydreamin in my favourite place beside the dam.

It had quickly filled up again and was, to me anyway, just the kind of place where fairies would live. I really did believe in them and I was sure I could sense them around me. The cycle of nature was fascinating too, with frogs' spawn turning into tadpoles, legs appearing, and finally these little creatures would be frogs too, and at a certain point in their growth they would disappear, leaving the dam once more to all the other wildlife. With all this magic around me it was easy to believe in fairies. Sitting by that dam all my troubles faded away and I felt I was living in heaven.

Chapter Ten
Coos an cars.

We hidna lang got ower the fire when Dad decided that the coo he had bought fae auld Pyper wis jist done, an wid hae tae ging tae the knackers' yard. Buying a new one would make a big hole in the budget. We only ever had one cow at a time at Fishermyre and provided it was a good one, it would supply us with enough milk, butter and cheese for our own use and a little extra.

Any other person would have gone to the local mart to buy a cow, but that would have meant Dad taking a day off his work, so he wid jist ging an see an auld frien o' his in Stoney. This man owned one of the garages in the town, some farms round about, and had his finger in other pies as well. He was the ideal person Dad thocht tae gie him a good deal on a coo. Fairmers aye hid tae feel they wir gettin a good deal an Fishermyre wis nae exception.

He came back fae Stoney lookin fair pleased wi himsel. This frien wid hae a braw milker delivered to us in a few days. The deal had been sealed wi the usual hand spittin an shakin. Now this deal wis made in this friend's garage in town an Dad hidnae seen the coo. He was a bit naïve at times.

The coo duly arrived aff the float an I could tell right away that Mum and Dad were far fae pleased. The coo wis broon ye see, an they hidna been expectin a broon coo. I didnae ken fit difference it made, bit Dad got the sharp side o' Mum's tongue for nae gaen tae see the coo afore he bocht it. Apparently she'd aye said yon mannie couldna be trusted. My Mum was really good at being wise after the event and to me it seemed an awfu fuss tae mak jist because the coo wis broon. I never did find out why they disliked brown cows so much. But there was more to the story than that. This coo was jist a rickle o' beens an didna look weel. So, trying to make the best of a bad deal, the cow was put into one of our best grass fields in the hope that she would improve.

However within a couple of days the cow had bad

diarrhoea and when the vet was called he diagnosed TB. This was another cow for the knacker's yard, with a vet's bill into the bargain. As soon as the vet left Dad was inta the auld Fordie an aff doon tae Stoney tae get his money back fae his frien. It wasn't a happy meeting and finally Dad insisted this man come up to Fishermyre and hae a look at this coo for himsel. He arrived shortly after in a very large new car wearing a soft hat, expensive suit and had on beautifully polished brown shoes. Noo ha'in broon shoes tae Mum and Dad was as bad as ha'in a broon coo. They thocht ye wir tryin tae be a bittie above yer station if ye hid broon shoes. (I haven't found the origins of this belief either).

Sensing trouble, Mum quickly disappeared into the house, but I marched behind the two men down to the field to help them inspect the cow. From the discussion that followed, I gathered that all responsibility was denied because Dad had bought the cow unseen, and this man wasn't prepared to give Dad any of his money back or exchange the cow for another one. There was quite a heated row, and I could see that my Dad wasn't winning. He had even lined the man up at the back of the cow so that he could see for himself that its ribs were sticking out along its back and that the beast was obviously far from healthy. At the height of the row, the coo slowly lifted its tail an Dad and I hid jist enough time tae jump smartishlike tae either side. The brave mannie, as Dad called him later, wisnae sae lucky. An arch o' skitter caught him richt doon his front a the wey tae the shiny broon shoes.

Dad an I didnae lauch, well, not then anyway. But we did leave him tae get intae his big car and drive off without any offer of help to clean up. Dad jist said "That bugger did me wi that coo". But I telt ye already there is a God in heaven and there was a little divine justice. The financial loss was huge for a small croft, but Dad made the most of the tale for a long time after, and I doubt that the expensive suit or brown shoes were ever worn again. The new car tae wid've taen a bit o' cleanin so Dad wouldn't have been the only loser.

This fall out between Dad and his friend was a bit

awkward because his was the garage we normally used. Dad had always been a horseman an kint naethin aboot cars. Takin the car to a garage wis a big thocht because they weren't easy to pay, an they wid aye find something else tae sort. This would have been quite genuine in our case because our cars were never serviced, nor would they have passed an MOT even if there had been such a thing. A new garage had to be found because Dad vowed that nae mair o' his money wis gaen into thon brave mannie's pooch.

The first repair needed after the broon coo episode was a welding job, and Dad was on his way home from another garage having had this done, when he realised something was burning inside the car. He stopped and found that the soft fluffy lining in the back was well alight. He leapt out but found there was nothing he could do but stand and watch while every scrap of the lining slowly burned to ash. To my surprise Dad didn't seem greatly put out by this event. I suppose since our cars rarely had any value anyway it didn't even occur to him to claim damages, and there was no question of changing the car. Efter a, it still hid an engine, so we jist used it as it wis wi the bare metal inside. It was a good story to tell though, and Dad made the most of that always ending with "Bit I gid back an telt the bugger".

Shortly after this, and believing that lightening never strikes the same place twice, our car went back to this same garage to have a new tyre fitted. On this occasion Dad made it home and was returning to work when, going down the Powbare, he saw a wheel speeding past. Almost at the same instant there was a lurch, a grinding noise and the car slew round and came to a halt blocking the road. It turned out that the bolts had not been tightened up when the wheel was put back on by the mechanic, and so it was only going to be a matter of time before they worked loose and came off. Dad of course could have been injured or even killed but he seemed mair pit oot by the fact that his wheel cairied on doon the brae, an he hid to walk a the wye doon for't and back up again tae pit it back on. Now he hid anither story tae tell. Bit maybe it wis time tae look for yet another garage. Between broon coos, burnin cars an wayward wheels, he wisna haen much luck wi garages.

Chapter Eleven.
Turkeys, jeuks an Christmas a get the go by.

Although Dad had a day job he got an enormous amount of work done on the croft in the evenings and at weekends and Mum was always right there helping him. In the summer months we worked until we were exhausted and then fell into bed. Even in winter a lot of jobs could be done with the light of the Hurricane Lamp. All our lighting, inside and out, was by paraffin with the lamp glasses cleaned daily. This was usually my job because my hands were small. Cold ashes from the fire were shaken around inside them, tipped out and then each glass was polished using elbow grease. The wicks were trimmed by Mum to ensure that the flame burned evenly, and after the lamps were topped up with paraffin they were ready to light up the darkness of another night.

We changed to a Tilley Lamp in the kitchen later on, and I bought this out of my first wages from tattie gathering at neighbouring farms. These lamps still burned paraffin but under pressure, and the really bright light came through a little mantle that I am told was made of silk. We were so excited about this new lamp that on the first night, Mum, Dad and I stood outside the house, looking in amazement through the window into the kitchen. We had never seen any paraffin lamp as bright as this one was. That was a good moment of togetherness I remember. From my tattie money too I sent telegrams to Sandy in the Far East just to say we were thinking about him. After a few he asked me to stop because he got scared to open them in case they were bringing bad news. I could understand that.

The scratchers had quickly got the go by and henhouses had appeared in their place. New materials were difficult if not impossible to get during the war so auld widd hid tae dae. Today it would be called reclaimed or recycled. Dad was very good at "acquiring" stuff but Mum did her bit here too. When a purchase had to be made, a very last resort I can tell you, after feeding all the animals and hens she would catch the bus early in the morning into Stonehaven. From there she took another bus to

Dundee. This was a long journey at that time with the bus stopping at houses and road ends all along the way. Arriving in Dundee she then made her way to Brands. Today this would be called a reclamation yard. With a list from Dad she would buy everything he needed, sometimes having little idea what the items were and if necessary taking whatever best fitted the description. Then the return journey had to be made, maybe having a quick cup of tea somewhere on the way. Back home all the evening chores would have to be tackled and a meal put on the table for Dad. Her purchases would be delivered by lorry a few days later. For someone who hated going far from home, this journey must have taken a lot of courage, but Mum would have done anything for Dad and I never saw her lacking in courage over serious things.

With new henhouses and sheds, Mum could now get down to the business of increasing the number of hens she kept for laying. Traditionally, on farms and crofts, the egg money was used for the housekeeping and it had to be very carefully managed to last through the times when the hens went aff the lay. Dad's wages, the envelope always handed over unopened, and income from the sale of animals, potatoes, grain and the like, met the outlays for restocking with animals for breeding or fattening, purchase of seeds and any second hand implements we needed. Buying anything new in the way of equipment rarely happened.

Mum kept a lot of leghorn hens, scrawny brown looking things they were, but good layers and not very fussy eaters. There seemed to be no ill will towards broon hens – only broon coos an shoes. But, copying other farms, she said she would like to have a go at rearing a few turkeys for the Christmas market or more probably New Year. Christmas wasn't celebrated much in Scotland at that time or certainly not around our way. Hogmanay night and into New Year's Day was the celebration time. Christmas Day wasn't even a holiday for people like us. Dad and everyone else worked on that day. You can imagine what that meant to a child. Santa Claus left me a piece of fruit, usually an apple, a small bar of chocolate, maybe a notebook and pencil, a ribbon for my hair perhaps and that was about it. Children in towns seemed to fare a little better with toys, but maybe that was just how I perceived it to be. Certainly as soon as I admitted that I knew there was no Santa Claus even these small gifts ceased. I'm sure for many other children it would have been the same, but I so longed for a proper Christmas.

On one occasion I was determined to have at least a Christmas tree, as I was sure ours was the only house in the country without one. I knew that wasn't true, but I was still of an age when I liked doing the poor me stuff. I went off to the wood and sawed down a small tree and set it up in the house, decorating it with bows made from scraps of fabric from the ragbag. I defied Mum and refused to take it down when she came in and saw it. When Dad came home that night she met him in the yard and told him the story. He strode in, picked up my tree and threw it on the rubbish heap. I don't remember Dad ever being really angry with me up until then. I thought my heart would break. Apparently even wanting a Christmas tree showed how "different" I was. Perhaps it wasn't as bad as it sounds and maybe it was just poor me stuff.

The apple in my stocking was a real treat because during the war years, fresh fruit was almost non-existent except for what grew locally. Nor would we have wanted our sailors to risk their lives for oranges, bananas and the like. I think I was about thirteen before I tasted a banana and I was none the worse for that. Sweets too were rationed and if we hadn't any coupons, we did have the option of taking some of our sugar ration to a shop and exchanging it for sweets. This never happened with us, because every grain of sugar was saved for baking and jam making. We had a wealth of wild fruit growing around us. Rasps, (they also grew in our garden along with gooseberries, strawberries and currants thanks to Lizzie Pyper) brambles and blaeberries were all picked nearby and made into something.

Mum got to be a dab hand at making wine and even made whisky. It was not from berries of course. Distilling whisky was against the law, but the bobbies were ower busy tae bother aboot Mum and a few bottles of home made whisky. On any of their frequent visits checking animal movements, they would quite likely have had a taste "jist tae try it". It had quite a kick I heard the grown ups say. Because of the toddy I was never tempted to taste it. I did have a taste of something else though. One day I found a bottle of White Lady cocktail in a cupboard when I was having a reenge aboot. I had a little taste and quite liked it, so I had a little more. Then I worried about being found out and filled the bottle up with water. Over the next week or so I finished that bottle of White Lady and I don't know at what point I stopped topping it up with water, but when it was completely empty I did refill the bottle with water and replaced it exactly where I had found it. One evening some time later some neighbours had dropped in for a crack and Dad decided to share the White Lady cocktail with them. "Jist tae try it", he said. As you can imagine I was a wee bittie worried, but by now I was too big to hide under the table so had to sit it out. The irony was, I wasn't offered any being considered too young tae be drinkin. On tasting the cocktail, there was great disappointment all round, but Dad jist said "Mither we've kept this bottle ower lang, its turned tae watter". They all had a good laugh and Mum got out her homemade brew. It was declared much better than thon shop bought rubbish. If only they had known!

So, as I said earlier, Mum would try her hand at being a turkey   farmer. Dad went to a lot of trouble to make the conditions for rearing the turkey chicks as favourable as possible. They needed extra heating, supplied by a lamp that had to be checked frequently on cold nights. That wis a richt scutter and then some of the chicks turned up their toes and died for no apparent reason. When big enough to be outside they didn't like the wet and some more died. Most of those left guzzled a lot of food, lapped up all the attention Mum could give them, and then they died. Maybe the turkeys just didn't like us and very quickly the feeling became mutual. After selling the few that survived, Mum declared "Bloody ill-natered beasts, we'll nae hae them again. I think we'll try jeuks."

Now we seemed to have ideal conditions for ducks with our own dam to swim in and plenty of places to roam. We paid a visit to a nearby farm to buy some duck eggs, and back home they were put under a clockin hen. Jeuks' eggs being bigger than hens' eggs wid fetch a better price, Mum thought. No time was wasted on market research, even if we had known what it was. I always loved to watch baby chicks and when they hatched, the baby ducklings were even better. They looked as if they had stepped right out of a cartoon at the pictures. The mother hen seemed a bit bewildered when, at only a few days old, her brood made straight for the dam whenever they could, swimming off and leaving her behind. Obviously she hidna been telt that her chicks were jeuks. A cruel deception I thought. Now as the little ducklings grew bigger and braver, mother hen got the go by altogether and they set off exploring on their own. No one had told my mother that jeuks were wanderers, an naebody hid telt the jeuks that they hid tae come hame at bedtime. We all spent hours at dusk tracking them down to any boggy bit on the moor they had taken a fancy to. Then they had to be got back to the croft and that was no easy job, before being safely tucked up for the night. Eventually when they were big enough to lay, we couldna find their eggs. This was common enough wi hens, but we were fly tae them an kent a their hidey-holes around the croft. Wi the jeuks it wis a different ball game. Their eggs could be anywhere, usually on the moor, an it got tae be that they jist wirna worth the bother. The jeuks hid tae go.

If nothing else my Mum was persistent and she next thocht "Fit aboot geese?" Now this time a feasibility study was done. She maybe didn't call it that of course, it was mair like "Ah'll hae a speir aboot". The answer she got back was that geese were a lot hardier than turkeys but even mair ill-natered. After that we stuck to chickens and as the flock was built up I spent quite a few hours a week after school wiping the eggs, sorting them by size and packing them ready to be picked up weekly by the Egg Marketing Board. There were worse jobs and Mum and I got on fine when we wir workin thegither.

Chapter Twelve
Makin dae.

As I have mentioned, money was short and that, together with a natural reluctance to spend it, led to Dad acquiring what he needed in different ways. Always was the belief that he could make whatever it was himself, or he could get it by barter and he certainly wasn't above asking around to see if anyone hid ane o' fitiver it wis he wis efter ga'in spare. If all else failed then money would have to change hands. A deal would be made with a spit on the hand afore "shakin on't". This exchange of body fluid meant that the deal was fair and honest and so were the people making it, or so Dad thocht. I've already said he was a bit naïve at times.

I liked his attitude though, because this readiness to make the best of any situation stood him in good stead most of the time. Making do and mending was the only way during the war anyway. Food, clothes and household goods were all rationed, with newly weds getting vouchers to allow them to buy furniture to set up home. For other people, some things were just impossible to obtain. This didn't bother us too much because we rarely did new anyway. Most things when they broke could be mended. There was actually a time when they were manufactured that way, unlike today. Mum never missed an opportunity to tell us how lucky we were to have so much of our own food and we undoubtedly were. We didn't live in clover though, that was for the cow. Mum rationed the eggs as after all they were her income, and any hen we did eat wid've qualified for the pension, bit still made a good pot o' soup..

Dad's favourite place to buy stuff wis at a ferm roup. Ony roup wid dae, but a ferm roup wis best. Roups meant a Seturday oot, ye picked up abody's crack (I mean gossip, that kind of crack) and so they were big occasions in Dad's life an ye didna hae tae need onything tae ging tae a roup. Ye could hae a richt reenge aboot amang a the stuff withoot onybody thinkin ye wir nosy, which he undoubtedly was. Man, it was almost yer duty to ging tae a roup. Mum sometimes went with him if she needed anything for the hens or the dairy, but mostly she stayed at home worrying how much Dad would spend, an jist fit wid he come hame wi this time. There appeared to be no restriction on spending at roups. On occasions he didn't even know what something he had bought was for. He wid say "Ach, naebody else wis biddin an it'll aye be eese for somethin". On one such occasion he came home with what was eventually identified as a wire-stretcher, bit that wis efter a lot o' speirin aboot. It had been in one of the mixed lots, and they were like magnets to men like my Dad. Of course the wire stretcher was eventually used. I never quite knew whether we actually needed the fence he put up using it. Wis it jist a ploy to prove his point aboot athing comin in handy some time, an so that he could play wi his new toy? Such was the madness that would take him over at a roup.

    Mum did her bit to economise too though. When she had enough feathers from the hens that ended up in the pot, she would make pillows, stuffing the feathers into casings made from recycled bleached flour bags. The good bits of old sheets were made into pillowcases. Caff was used for stuffing mattresses and this was changed often. It took a whilie to get comfortable in a newly filled caff bed an it didna half mak ye sneeze. Dad's working boots were lined with straw to keep his feet warm in winter and absorb any sweat in summer. This straw would be changed on a Sunday night ready for another working week. Although Mum and I found our wellies awfu cauld on our feet, we were never tempted to take Dad's advice and stuff them with straw. He wis on his own wi that ane.

    Absolutely nothing was wasted. When rugs were worn and the backing showed through, they would be painted with fabric dye to make them look a bittie better. These rugs would have been of pretty poor quality when new, as they were usually bought from passing tinkers. Mum always said that she only bought things at the door because she felt sorry for the tinkers, but I think she was also just a little nervous of them. We never quite knew whether to believe the stories of the evil eye or not. I did sometimes find little stones arranged outside the gate after a tinker had just left, and we believed this was a message to others passing by about how we had treated them. It was considered better to keep on the right side of them by always buying something, whether ye were needin it or no, jist in case. Mum was really quite superstitious and she also believed in the supernatural. That wasn't often spoken about of course.

In the winter evenings we made clootie rugs. Dad made the frame from auld widd. With a file he fashioned the hooks from cutlery, then he gave them a well smoothed wooden handle. A washed hessian sack was opened out and tacked on to the frame and using a wax crayon one of us would draw a design on the hessian as a rough guide. With a pile of rags cut or torn into narrow strips we were ready to start. The frame, being the full size of the rug, was balanced on our knees and we all worked on the rug together, while listening to the wireless. It was a special treat to be allowed to put in the last few loops to finish a rug. Another piece of hessian was sewn on to the back to finish the rug off. These rugs were very heavy, lay on the floor beautifully and nowadays would be considered quite suitable to hang on a wall.

A newly made clootie rug went into one of the bedrooms, usually over the bottom of the bed to keep our feet warm. We didn't have heating in any room other than the kitchen and we went to bed with a stone pig in winter to keep warm. The heat from this lasted until morning. Mercy on us if we let it fa oot o' the bed fin abody wis asleep, for the din wid've waukened the deid. The rug that had been replaced on the bed would go down on the floor. The bedroom floor rugs made their way to the kitchen, then, cut or folded in half, to the outside doorstep and finally the filthy muddy one would go on the rubbish heap to rot away. Recycling was our way of life an we thocht naethin o't.

Of all the shortages, petrol rationing hit us hardest. Dad had given up contracting for the Forestry Commission and now worked in the sawmill just down the road. The mill was very near to the croft and Dad could have cycled to work. After all, wasn't he the one who was always telling us that he had biked along every road in Aberdeenshire in his young day, but bikin' aboot on roads noo wouldn't have done Fishermyre's image any good, so he always took the car using up our precious ration of petrol. (That was only my opinion of course.) With hindsight maybe I was a bit hard on my Dad for he was getting even more "as ready tae row's rin" as the years passed, but I loved going to the pictures and visits only happened when there was enough petrol to spare.

I can only think of one drawback to our visits to the picture house. After the episode of the beasties in my hair earlier on, I had a mortal dread o' beasties o' ony kind. In the picture house it was quite likely that I wid pick up at best a flech, at worst a married flech wi a kjarn o' bairns. Their bites brought me out in great red weals.

Halfway through the evening the usherette at the pictures would come round and spray us all with Flit. This was supposed to kill off any bugs, and even though it made my eyes nip, that was still better than gaen hame wi a flech.

One evening, it was announced that we had enough petrol, so a trip to the pictures it would be. Apart from the obvious enjoyment of the films, my Mum and Dad liked to see the Pathe News to keep up to date with the latest on the war. Reading the papers or listening to the radio was all right, but actually seeing the news was much better.

Now we didn't pay any heed to when films would start or finish. We went in when convenient, most often in the middle of one of the films and sat round until it came to the bit we'd already seen, and then we would leave. It was all so simple. Having seen the ending of a mystery before the beginning didn't spoil our enjoyment one little bit. My, we wir easy pleased.

So we set off and duly arrived at The Picture House car park in Stonehaven. It was in darkness of course because of the blackout. Getting out of the car we all heard a soft "cluck". We listened and there it was again "cluck, cluck". Then there was a flutter. In the dip between the bonnet and the mudguard sat one of Mum's hens, looking very bewildered and bedraggled in the light from our flashie. Earlier, when Dad had arrived home from the sawmill, this hen must have roosted on the car for the night. With the warmth from the engine she had mistaken it for a safe place to be. How was she to guess that shortly she would be bowling off to the pictures? My mother was in no doubt what needed to be done. "We canna afford to lose a hen", she said. "If it hid been a cock maybe, but nae a hen. Onywye, this is ane o' ma best layers. Na, na we'll jist hae tae ging hame an hope this disnae pit her aff the lay". Now of course I was aware that my mother's priorities somewhat differed from mine, but just in case, I tried "Let's thraw its neck and hae't for oor denner the morn". That little remark didn't go down too well. I wis jist ga'en tae hae tae miss the pictures.

Greatly disappointed we all piled back into the Fordie and headed home. The hen was plonked on my knee in the back with orders to "Hud on tult". Now three miles is a long way with a hen on your knee and there was worse to come. I discovered one of my Dad's little secrets that night.

On reaching the sawmill where he worked, he stopped, got an empty petrol can from the boot and disappeared over the dyke into the sawmill yard, calling back as he went, "Ah winna be lang, I'm jist ga'en tae siphon aff a drappie petrol. If the bobbies come by, say ah'm awa for a pee". An there's me sittin' wi a hen on ma knee. Being disappointed and in a huff I shouted efter im "Dad this hen's peckin' me fae ae end an shitin' on me fae the ither". He jist turned his head, laucht an shouted "Hud yer wheesht quine, pit yer fit on't, a winna be lang".

Coming back he hid the can, now full of petrol, in the boot and I realised how he could, now and again, find the petrol to take us to the pictures. Could this be why he had to take the car to work, he couldna cairry a can o' petrol on a bike.
Anither night, again when Dad jist managed to spare a drappie petrol, we landed up at the picters and this time we did actually see the films, bit on the wye hame we ran doon a rabbit. This wis quite a surprise tae me for at the speed o' the auld Fordie, ony self-respecting rabbit surely could've shifted itsel. It got thrown in the back wi me an a, but it, unlike the hen, we *wid* hae

for oor denner next day. Unfortunately for me it had only been stunned and quickly came to life jumping all over me in the back seat. Dad jist laucht at that tae, bit he didna lauch lang fin the stink got up, and he realised the car wis ga'en tae need a good clean. I wisna ga'en tae dae't I telt im, because, besides ha'en a rabbit dumped on ma knee, I wis still in the huff ower the business o' the hen.

Betty 1938

Sandy, Gladys and Teddy. Late 1930's

Mum and Dad Smith – late 1930's

Alfie as a Dispatch Rider in
West Africa about 1941

Sandy as a Dispatch Rider in Burma
about 1941

Betty 1949

L. to R. Wullie, Violet. Teddy, Joyce, Cathie
and Alfie, 1949

Chapter Thirteen.
Tam – couthie cratur or coorse?

As soon as we took over the croft we needed power to work the land. With Dad's long experience of horses in his ferm servant days it wid be horsepower that we wid go for, he said. Nae tractors for us, an horses were cheaper, which was probably the real reason. So in aboot the ferm toon came Tam. How he was acquired I never knew and I still to this day really don't care.

I did know that Tam had done a milk round in Stoney for many years before coming to blight my life. That horse gave every one of us hell, except Dad, and Mum of course, for she swore she wouldn't go near the brute - ever. Wise woman, but she hid a choice.

At first Dad worked Tam himself, but you grow up quickly on a croft with so much work to be done. There were so few hours of daylight in winter and Dad had his full time job. It wasn't long before we had a repeat of the headmistress thing, "If she's big enough, she's old enough" except that it would have been more like Dad saying, "Bett's a gallus quine, she'll manage Tam fine". I wasn't sure I liked my description of "gallus quine" much, but from Dad it was a compliment. Receiving any compliments, even backhanded ones from Dad was to be treasured, for he didna mak a habit o' dishin them oot.

He did teach me a few words of horsey speak before I went near Tam. Apparently "hie" wasn't meant to be a friendly greeting, but an instruction to Tam to turn left. Then there was a "hup", an a "hish" cam intae it somewey, but the only ane Tam kint wis "wo" which meant stop. I didnae bother learnin them a. There just didn't seem any point. Between Tam an me I kint fa wis boss, an it wisnae me.

Tam was the maist ill-gitted, coorse beast I have ever encountered. He was sleekit tae, maken on he wis couthie and biddable when Dad wis aboot, then showing his true nature wi Teddy and me. Dad said he was a work pony. The word "work" didn't ever come into any description of Tam used by the rest of us. Dad said he had rescued him from ending up in a tin of dog food. I had to wrestle hard with my conscience not to wish he had.

If you can cast your mind back, you may remember that I didn't like horses, big or little, Clydesdale or work pony. At least I was too old now to be thrown on their backs, and being big enough to wear dungarees, the knicker flashing part of my life was long gone. However when I was sent to bring Tam in from the field to be harnessed up, I was still somewhat vertically challenged compared to him, and so was at a disadvantage. He just needed to throw his head in the air and I had no hope of reaching his mane to put his halter on. After doing this to me a few times, I would shout for Dad, and as soon as he appeared, Tam would walk quietly up to him and give him a nuzzle as if to say "She only had to ask".

Tam's life doing the milk round in Stonehaven must have been idyllic, for at least once a fortnight he would run away and head back that way. Obviously he hadn't been told about the tinned dog food scenario. Dad, as I have already said, was on the plumpish side, so it isn't hard to guess who was always sent off to bring Tam back. I had no hope of catching up with him unless I took my bike, but then that made it difficult to lead him back home. Sometimes I was able to take a short cut through a field and head him off, and on occasions a kind farmer driving home from the town would stop and bar his way, allowing me to catch up. Indeed as you can guess, I never had any great desire to catch Tam, except that the further away he got, the further I then had to walk him back along the main road, with him snorting and glowering at me. He wasn't above giving me the odd nip with his teeth either, if I let my guard drop. As soon as we came into the yard and he saw Dad, he would put on the couthie cratur act again.

Teddy's first experience with Tam was no better than mine had been. Working with him in a field one day, come lowsin time, Teddy jumped up on his back for a ride home. Now what Teddy didn't know was that Tam had never suffered this indignity in his life before. He bolted up the road to the croft with Teddy just managing to hang on. Down the yard Tam sprinted, straight to the old bath used as a water trough, where he lowered his head and deftly tipped Teddy into it, before trotting off to the stable on his own. After that it was war between them as well, and at last I had an ally tae curse an swear wi aboot Tam.

Dad had made a neat little float for Tam to pull, and even I could see that he had made a really nice job of it. It was kept in a shed, and Tam had to be harnessed up and then backed into it while the shafts were up. When I did this I had to judge just the right spot for Tam to stand, so that when I lowered the shafts a leather strap would fit perfectly into the groove on Tam's saddle. I would do it all so carefully, but just as I lowered the shafts, Tam would take one step forward an stan there grinnin at me, and I would have to start lining him up all over again. After a few goes at it, I would have to get Dad to help. This manoeuvre was easy for a grown up, because they could guide Tam backwards with one hand and lower the shafts with the other. Having to do it in two manoeuvres gave Tam the chance tae mak a fool o' me, although he niver took the len o' Dad.

Although I had to do many jobs around the croft with Tam, I was never allowed to plough. Dad did that himself. I was saved from ploughing by Dad's liking for straight furrows, particularly when they could be seen from the road. I didn't do straight anything and I didn't do neat either, but after all Dad had his reputation to maintain and didn't he used to enter ploughing matches afore he came up in the world? Na, na ploughin couldna be trusted tae a quine, gallus though she wis. I couldn't have agreed more.

But sadly the harrowing could, and all of it was my job. Now when with me Tam only worked if it pleased him and mostly it didn't. He would work away fine when we were heading towards the gate and home, but as soon as we turned away to do another strip he stopped and wouldn't budge. This was when I would have to dig into my pockets for one of the many slices of bread I kept hidden there to entice him to continue. I've seen Mum even having to bring out more bread, just so that I could get a field finished afore Dad came home. Oh, how I hated that horse. Later on when Sandy came back from Japan after the war had ended, he joined Teddy and me in this hate campaign. I think Sandy fared worse than I did wi Tam, for I had picked up a few sneaky tips of my own tae get him tae work.

Tam seemed tae ging through a lot o' shoes. Maybe it wis a that runnin awa doon the road that did it, but I would, too often, have to spend a Saturday morning walking him the three miles into Stoney to the blacksmith. The first time I did this I was taken by surprise. What I didn't know was that as soon as we hit the town we were on his old milk round. So what happened? Tam stopped at every house along the way that he used to deliver milk to. Some of his old customers came out to make a fuss of him, giving him piecies and petting him, while he stood there doing his couthie cratur hard done by act. I stood helpless and ignored looking on, for Tam would only move when he wanted to. I'm sure if he could have spoken, he would have told everyone that I beat him every day, an me only half the height o' him. At one point he spied the water trough on the other side of the street and made a beeline for it, with me chasing after him. I swear he tried to judge the distance so that he could make it safely, but with the hope that I didn't. Such, I am sure was how his mind worked.

These journeys to the smiddy were very embarrassing for me. I prayed that no one from my class at school would see me. To be seen in dungarees leading a horse through the town would never be lived down. I would be a laughing stock. I would hide while the blacksmith shod Tam, which took a wee while, and then I would head home and hope to clear the town with him without being spotted. Once on the country road I could relax a bit. With luck no one would have seen me in ma dungers in the toon wi a horse.

Chapter Fourteen
Neeps, tatties an the hairst.

Crofting sounds such a good way of life and in the early
years I really enjoyed it, but after school and at weekends I was
expected to work and work hard. This alone set me aside from
the other children at school. I couldn't go into town and do what
they did. It never occurred to me that they might be bored. I
imagined my classmates having a wonderful life. The grass
always appears greener, but in reality I know it seldom is.

Most Saturdays in the winter I was expected to go oot an
pu' neeps. When the ground was hard with frost I needed the
hook on the tapner to get them from the frozen ground, and then
two flicks with the blade part topped and tailed them. Enough
turnips had to be pulled to last the animals for a week. After that
was done I then had to persuade my enemy Tam to get between
the shafts of the float, and stay there long enough for me to get it
roadit. Then it was off to the field, load all the pu'd neeps and
home and into the shed wi them. Each evening after school I had
to slice enough turnips for a day's feed. This was done with a
thing like a guillotine and was really hard to do if the neeps
hadn't fully thawed out, and was often done in the freezing cold
by the light from a paraffin lamp. Some nights my hands were
so cold I would hardly have noticed if I'd sliced off the tip of a
finger.

Come the milder weather the turnip seed had to be sown
for another crop. This was never trusted to me as it involved
straight dreels that could be seen from the road. Tattie planting I
did do though, with Mum and anyone else who could be coerced
into helping. I didn't enjoy the work, but there was a closeness
between us when we all worked together that I liked very much.
During these times I didn't feel so different, and I didn't have to
try so hard to please.

After seed sowing Fishermyre would enjoy a stroll round
his land in the evenings, waiting for the neeps and oats to breer
or the tatties tae get thru the grun. He would come back and tell
Mum with excitement in his voice, that the neeps were thru an

that it wis a good breer. If the tatties came through a bit earlier than he had calculated, he would worry about a late frost nipping the soft growth. Fermin was a dicey business he would say, but there wis nae doobt he wis a fermer at heart and he wis now in his richtfu place.

When it came to the thinning of the turnips, a long, back breaking, boring task, I really let myself down. I was hopeless at it. With a Dutch hoe the seedlings had to be weeded and thinned out leaving the width of the hoe between the plants, to allow them room for growth. I had rather long gaps in my rows due to my lack of skill, and I would transplant a few seedlings here and there to cover up my mistakes. After a day of sunshine these seedlings would die and Dad would easily see which rows were mine. I always hoped he wouldn't let me back and he always hoped I would improve. It was a no win situation for both of us.

In the autumn the tatties were lifted and pitted up, usually at the edge of the field they had been grown in, and as near the gate as possible. This involved a deep covering of straw to keep the frost out and then earth piled on top. We tried not to go into the pits during the hardest weather for obvious reasons. Pitting the tatties was Dad's job, but before they got to that stage they had to be lifted. Tattie gathering was very much a part of our lives and I earned pocket money working at the other farms round about. At first I would have a "half bit". This was just as it sounds. The length of the field was divided up into "bits" according to the number of gatherers. A very long field would be done in two halves. Until I grew bigger half a bit was all I could keep up with and even that took a bit o' doing. We started very early in the morning and we wouldn't have dreamt of being late for yokin time. On a small farm the farmer's wife would bring out hot tea, scones and pancakes at piecie time. Lunch would be provided in the farm kitchen and we would get a hurl on the bogey to save time getting there, even sittin on the back o' a hard bouncin bogey wis a treat efter bein bent double a mornin. Lunch or denner as we called it, usually started with soup, often broth, that everyone else seemed to enjoy, so I pretended that I liked it too. This was followed by a meat and vegetable course, served always in the unwashed soup plate to avoid too much washing up. I struggled a bit wi the unwashed plate, but it wis a common practice an we did it at hame a the time. The struggle I had eating from an unwashed plate wis supposed to be another reason why I was different. My mother blamed this being different for onything she didna like aboot me. The afternoon piecie would be tea, more scones and cake. We were really well looked after and of course all the piecies were home baked.   Pity the reputation of a farmer whose wife served anything bought from a shop. That wid've caused a richt speik, an nae fermer winted tae be the ane tae cause a speik. Funny tae think that a man's reputation wid hing on his wife's baking skills.

As I got older and could take on a full bit, I would cycle to Stonehaven and catch a lorry as part of a squad gathering potatoes further afield. The pay was much higher, the work even harder and no dinner or piecies provided, home baked or otherwise. We were often hashed and would even go on strike. To be hashed meant the digger would come round too fast for us to have had time to finish gathering our bit. We spent a lot of time at the bigger farms praying that the digger would break down, but the farmer would see to it that it seldom did.   I remember feeling very brave when I went on strike, but I only did it once, because the penalty was never being able to go back to that particular squad again. Not too far from us up Rickarton way, was a POW camp and the men from there shared our work. The prisoners were usually Italian and we all liked working with them. They were kind to us and helped us when we struggled. When we had a good friendly squad none of us would stop gathering when we reached our own marker. We helped each other to finish, so that we might all get a few minutes rest until the digger came round again. The Italian POWs were more than generous with their help and I cannot speak too highly of them.

Our only grain crop was oats, always called corn, and after the fields had been prepared, me daein the harrowing bit hindered by Tam, Dad would sow the seed. He would strap the happer (a large shallow canvas tray) around him, fill it with corn and set off with measured strides. The corn was scattered first by one hand then the other in rhythm. I loved watching this because it looked so simple, but I knew Dad kept his concentration, never altering the length of his stride, his speed or the hand movements. Only when the oats breered would we see how evenly he had done the job. Mum and I had to refill the happer at intervals with pails of seed, Dad never moving from his spot in case he missed a bit.

Apart from pu'in up a few skelloch plants over the summer from amongst the grain I had nothing to do with it until endrig clearing time. An overabundance of skelloch in your fields wis likely tae cause another speik so it fell to me to uphold Fishermyre's reputation as a fermer by keepin on tap o't.

When the grain was ripe the endrigs had to be cleared to allow the binder space to turn. Dad cut this grain with a scythe and Mum and I followed behind, gathering it into sheaves and tying it up with a band made from a few stems of the corn. I was useless at this as well and I blamed the midgies, its awfu handy tae hae somethin tae blame. It wis a richt for Dad, he smoked his Bogey Roll filled pipe, an puffed awa at that. One whiff o' it an the midgies made a bee line for Mum an me. In spite of splashing citronella all over ourselves, we wid be covered in swollen lumps by the end of an evening, life wisna very fair sometimes.

Later we followed the binder setting the sheaves up into stooks. Ah wisna good at that either, my stooks aye fell doon. Maybe I let my mind wander tae the braw time abody else wis ha'in in the toon, nae stookin for the ither quines in my class. When the sheaves had dried and were ready for stacking, I had tae big the cairt while Mum and Dad forked the sheaves up tae me. Now, I dinna like heights, or things that shoogle fin I'm on tap o' them. I didna trust Tam nae tae rin aff wi me, an I dinna dae neat. My qualification for biggin floats wis that there wisna onybody else.

When the float was loaded I couldn't get off it, because although I was scared of being up there, I was even more terrified of trying to get down. I would spreadeagle myself on top of the load and hang on until we got into the farmyard and I could fork the sheaves over to Dad to build them. I wis jist thankfu I wisna expected tae build the stacks, bit then I widna hae been, for they were next the road. I wis allowed tae mak a wee decoration wi the corn to finish aff the taps though. They wir kinda like a crown if I remember rightly, an Dad liked to wear a little corn dolly in his buttonhole at hairst times. He liked the auld customs, an foo nae?

Since Dad had scorned the hame made affair o' a thrashin mull, he had to hire the use of one for a day to thresh the corn for us. This day was a big event in our year. Once the day was set, neighbours had to be told. The required number would give Dad a day's labour and in return he would do the same for each of them. That was the only way crofts and small farms could work and it was a friendly system that worked very well.

The hired mill was powered by a steam engine and as the mill had to be positioned near the stacks, there was no way the engine could get into the yard as well. It straddled the minor road beside the croft completely blocking it. A massive belt linked the engine and the mill. It looked very, very dangerous to be near and should never have been on a public road, but Health and Safety hadn't been heard of. All the neighbours knew Fishermyre would be threshing on that day, so they would make a detour if needbe to get into town. This happened every year and there was never a single complaint.

The first two years that we had the threshing mill everything went smoothly, but the third year when I was twelve or thirteen Dad was a man short. Two men were needed tae lowse and Dad only had one. Lowsin wis done at the top of the mill and involved cutting the binder twine on the sheaves before feeding them through the mill. Dad decided and announced to the others "We're a man short an Bett'll hae tae dae". The others argued a bit with Dad and said "Wullie, ye canna pit a lassie on tap o' a mull". Dad jist said "She's a gallus quine, she'll dae't fine". I can still remember how scared I was that day. The knife was very sharp and the strap wouldn't fit my small hand, I was shaking with nerves but the mill shook more, so the state I was in wasn't noticed. I kept up with the men as best I could, and Mum told me later that Dad got quite a few compliments about the gallus quine at the end of that day, bit it wid niver hae done for him tae hae telt me.

Chapter Fifteen
Sausage sizzles an porkers

Although I had now moved on to the Mackie Academy and was happier there, I still envied the girls who lived in the town. I particularly envied the ones who had been able to choose their own future. I had always wanted to work in a chemist's shop when I left school, and I was very disappointed when I was made to take a commercial course at the Academy, equipping me to work in an office. Mum and Dad had agreed this was a good idea because Mum said, "Ye can mak somethin o' yersel in an office". No one from our family had ever worked in an office except for Gladys, and she had lasted one week in the buroo in Aiberdeen. I wid like tae say that gettin the sack wisna her fault but it wis. Ye canna tell onybody that they stink o' fish an hope tae keep yer job. Gladys just laughed about it, but I could see that Mum and Dad were disappointed. There was no doubt they thought this choice of career was good for me, but I felt that if I was old enough to do a man's job on the croft, I should be considered old enough to choose what I wanted to do with the rest of my life.

Although I had to give in over this, I was determined to win another much less important battle. I had seen some of my classmates in their Girl Guide uniforms after school and I desperately wanted to be in the Guides too. I knew little of what the Guide movement stood for, and even less about what they actually did at their meetings, but I had made up my mind, I would be a Girl Guide like the others.

I had quite a few mountains to climb over this decision, the main one being that the Guide Leader didn't want me. Who could blame her? Come winter, I would have to cycle the three miles back to Stoney in the evenings and home again in all weathers. This was her main objection. We all see things as we wish to see them, and the picture I was getting was somewhat different to hers. I saw long balmy summer evenings, learning to tie beautiful knots and having sausage sizzles outdoors. I wasn't allowed to cook anything at home in case I wasted food and we only ate beef, lamb and poultry. A pork sausage to me would be a luxury indeed. Cooked and eaten outside too. Farming families didn't do picnics at that time. Why would we? In the summer we were never in, and what were picnics to others were "piecie times" to us. Of course this wisdom only came with hindsight.

After I had persuaded the reluctant Guider to accept me, I had a wall of opposition to get through at home. My next problem was where I was going to get the money for a uniform? I solved that by doing a bit of "speirin aboot" at school, and to my great excitement, a friend of a classmate gave me an outgrown uniform. It was so kind of her and answered my prayers. It didn't fit of course, anywhere, but hey what was new about that? I was now one of "them" and about to do toonser stuff.

I have to admit my Guide evenings were a tiny bit of a let down. I certainly did learn how to tie different knots, but then I did that on the croft anyway. Perhaps I should be more grateful though because years later my skill in knot tying turned into the craft of macrame. I taught this in evening classes around Angus, and my students won prizes at the Rural Show for their work. Was that seed sown in me all those years before?

As it was summer we had outings to Dunnottar Woods and places, to learn country things. The saying "Carrying coals to Newcastle" comes readily to mind, but we were promised that if we passed our fire lighting badge, we would have an evening walk in the country followed by a sausage sizzle. Now this was what I had been waiting for. When it came to my turn to sit my test, I had to light my fire in the Dunnottar Woods in pouring rain. I passed my badge that night, but didn't really see the point of it all. In the country we were very careful about fires and would never have lit one in a wood for such a frivolous purpose. I didn't tell the Guide Leader that, but I was a bit disillusioned. Of course I was overlooking the fact that all our fires were lit on our own land to burn tattie shaws or sometimes whins and old straw.

The big night of the sausage sizzle arrived, and I set off cycling the three miles to town with my pack of pork sausages and whatever else I needed. We were told that the Leader knew a kind farmer who would let us have the use of a field to build a fire and cook our food. What excitement for me, I was doing the same things as other girls did and at last I felt one of them.

We set off from the Guide Headquarters walking back up the Netherley road. We turned down the side road, we passed Fishermyre and stopped at Betty's Croft. This was to be our picnic spot. Can you imagine my disappointment? This was a field I had harrowed, planted, and harvested and that year it just happened to be in grass. The sausage sizzle no longer had the appeal I expected. The final irony of course was that I had to walk back to Stoney to get my bike, for I didn't fancy getting up early enough the next morning to walk to school. By the end of the evening I had biked six miles and walked another six to eat a few sausages in one of our own fields. For the rest of my life I have had a feeling of disappointment whenever I have eaten a sausage.

After that episode I didn't last long in the Guides. My initial enthusiasm had worn off, and the Guide Leader needn't have worried, I never did bike to Stoney in the dark evenings, not for the Guide meetings anyway. The grass on the other side was never quite as green again. The skills I learned from Mum and Dad living and working on the croft far exceeded anything I could be taught in the town.

The big question for me though was, had the kind farmer really given his permission for his field to be used? Dad was very quiet on that subject and I never did find out. He could be as devious as Tam sometimes.

A sausage sizzle may have been a dream of mine because we never ate bacon or pork, but that didn't stop us keeping pigs. We always had a few breeding sows and their large litters, after being fattened up, gave a good income. We did keep calves too, and during the war Mum had a strange belief that if she called the young calves after my brothers who were in the Forces, as long as the calves thrived, so would Alfie and Sandy. This belief scared me a bit, but she was quite adamant that it was true, and so we all cared for these calves before any of the other animals on the croft. Perhaps this helped Mum cope better with the separation from her laddies for there was no doubt she suffered great anguish while they were at war.

The pigs took less effort to rear than the calves. The sows had a sty each, and a little place to sun themselves on a good day. We always had plenty of fresh straw for them to lie on, and Mum boiled up their food in a big boiler in one of our many hoosies. By the time their litters of piglets were ready to be born the sows were pretty inactive, ate a lot, but were not at all fussy about their menu. Although it is a common belief that pigs are dirty animals, this really isn't so. They loved it when their sty had just been cleaned and given fresh straw. It was Dad's work to care for the pigs apart from feeding them. Some breeds could be very bad tempered and I was glad I was never expected to muck out. After a litter was born though, I did have to help. Because of the sheer bulk of a sow, it was difficult for her to lie down without squashing the odd piglet and each one was worth hard cash. To prevent accidents Dad always built a temporary low fence around the inside of the sty. This provided somewhere for the piglets to rush under when the sow showed signs of wanting to lie down for a doze or to let them feed. This worked reasonably well during the day, but for the first few nights Dad and I took turns at sitting up in the pigsty all night to keep the young ones safe. This was not my favourite way to spend the wee small hours I can tell you, and being half-asleep in class the next day wasn't much fun either. I hardly think I could have used the excuse that I had spent half the night in the pigsty.

One night when Dad was on duty he must have nodded off, and one piglet got squashed pretty flat. He immediately rescued it, and in desperation patted it back into shape, fully expecting to have to bury the poor thing in the morning. Its bones though were still soft, it survived the night, and although it was always the runt of the litter, it did grow to a reasonable size, but that little piggy didn't go to market with all the others.

During the war and for a time after, very strict records had to be kept of the movement of all farm animals, and were regularly checked by the police. This was to prevent farmers selling into the black market. Dad had been asked by butchers often enough to let them have a pig, but although tempted, had never broken the rules. On one occasion he succumbed. It was just at the end of the war and this butcher had been asked to supply pork for "some do or other". Social activities were just starting up again. He came to the croft and butchered our little runt. For Dad this didn't go as smoothly as he expected, for he discovered that he was quite fond of the little piggy whose life he had saved, and he didn't enjoy seeing it butchered. Although he got a very good price for the pig, I'm not sure that he considered this deal worth it. Mum and I were told tae bide in the hoose oot o' the road and I was sworn to secrecy over the black market piggy. I now did all the form filling work needed to do with the running of the croft, and I knew that of this litter I had entered that one piglet had died, as indeed it nearly had.

A few days after this, Dad came home from the town in a state of great agitation. Unknown to him the butcher's "some do or other" turned out to be none other than the first Police Ball after the war, and at the dinner preceding this our piggy had been the main course. According to Dad word wis a roon the toon that the butcher hid got hud o' a pig fae somewye. Dad sweated a bit over it all, and swore that wis the first an last o' that caper, it jist wisnae worth the risk. But why would the bobbies be interested? Hid they themselves nae destroyed the evidence?

Chapter Sixteen
Peace at last an catchin up wi the femily

The war came to an end in 1945, first VE Day and later VJ Day. Now, my brothers could come home. Sandy we missed most because being in the Far East we hadn't seen him in years.

On VE Day I was allowed into Stoney to celebrate. I joined a crowd of strangers and danced in the Market Square and surrounding streets well into the night. Most likely there was alcohol drunk, but even those of us without it were all drunk with relief, excitement and joy. It was a night never to be forgotten.

Patriotically all the women wore clothes in red, white and blue. I had a red blouse, blue skirt and white cardigan. These were hand me downs and had come in a parcel from Canada to a school friend and didn't fit her. I was delighted to have fallen heir to them and added them to my small wardrobe. I felt very grown up and smart. After dancing until exhausted, I had the three-mile journey home to make, but there were no rows that night for being late. We repeated the whole celebration later when Japan surrendered.

When both wars ended we expected to see the last of petrol coupons, food rationing and such like, but this didn't happen overnight. It was in fact years before we saw the end of rationing. I remember I was so looking forward to tasting a banana and even more so to the return of Stork margarine. All through the war I heard the grown ups say how wonderful it would be to have Stork back again. I didn't remember the taste of it because I had been so young when the war started, so I believed all I heard about Stork and looked forward eagerly to this treat. When it eventually did appear on the shelves again, I can't describe my disappointment, what a let down that was. My taste buds were accustomed to our own freshly churned butter, with Fishermyre stamped on it, on homemade bannocks and eaten with a chunk of Mum's wonderful cheese. No factory made margarine could compete with that.

Alfie of course was still serving in the Air Force when the war ended but he was stationed in Glasgow. He had married his Cathie and visited her unofficially every weekend. With no travel pass for the train and with other things to spend his service pay on, he would travel without a ticket, and would leap from the train as it slowed down, but just before it came in to Stonehaven Station. Down the railway embankment he went, on to the road and there he was in Brickfield where Cathie lived and was waiting for him. In this way he avoided the ticket collector. The end of the war eventually brought his demob, and he and Cathie could at last build their future together, having Cathie as a sister-in-law was very good for me. She was one of the nicest kindest people I have ever known and I valued her friendship very much. Theirs was a very happy home where I always felt welcome. I went round to Cathie's for lunch on weekdays for quite some time, and it was amazing the meals she could produce in spite of food rationing. Mum would give her eggs from our hens to eke out their rations and Cathie would preserve any she could spare in waterglass for the times when they were scarce. I remember too when she made either wine or ginger beer, bottled it, and stored it on the floor under the bath until it matured. One night, while the family was asleep the corks started popping, one after another, hitting the metal bath with a cacophony of sound, and wakening everyone in the house and probably the neighbours next door as well. Their three children were all born in the James Mowat Nursing Home. This was a private home and so had to be paid for. I think Mum and Dad were very proud of this. Mum certainly telt abody that wid listen tae her where her grandchildren were born.

Wullie being older and in a reserved occupation didn't do war service but his wife Violet had been busy having more babies. He had bought the bombed croft Birdieknap, built a new house there and raised seven children. Their home was the total opposite to ours. With all that had to be done on the croft, housework took a back seat with my mother. Of Violet, Mum would say "Ye could eat aff her fleer". I remember too, Violet baked the most wonderful Victoria sponges and always had a couple filled with jam and cream for any visitors.

Wullie's youngsters were a wild bunch with so much space to run around in, and having a very happy go lucky father. Discipline wasn't a high priority with my brother. Wullie and I got on well together and he would have given you anything except money, for he never had any. He spent most of his life being self-employed, and he was no businessman, so I greatly respected how Violet managed to make ends meet over the years. Wullie was very free with lifts in his lorry into Stoney though. It was probably a bit unusual to sit in the passenger seat of any lorry and watch the road speed by under your feet. Wullie's lorries often had no floor, and any passenger had to sit with their feet perched on either side of a hole. On reflection perhaps that is why I was the only one of the family who accepted lifts from him. Like all my bikes, his lorries had very little in the way of brakes either. Going down a hill, he would force the lorry into the lowest gear and drive with two wheels on the verges to slow him down a bit. Yes, it was always exciting to get a hurl in one of Wullie's lorries, dangerous maybe, but exciting.

After the birth of their last baby Violet and he realised that they were falling behind with the christenings. To catch up, and to save the embarrassment of having the last few children christened together in the church in front of a congregation, it was decided to ask the minister to come to the house.

The day of the christening was very hot and sunny and the window of the living room, where they also had their meals, was pushed up from the bottom for fresh air. With the christening over, the minister was invited to stay for a ham and salad meal. Violet also had a beautifully iced christening cake as a centrepiece on the table. The bairns were sent outside until the grown ups had eaten, and they all raced round to the front of the house and knelt out of sight under the open window, heads bobbing up and down keeping a close watch on how much food would be left for them. There was particular excitement when the grown ups reached the christening cake stage. This was the treat they were all waiting for.

The cake was duly cut and pieces handed round. The minister appeared to enjoy it immensely, and just as Violet offered him a second helping, a loud in drawing of breaths could be heard, and a louder "The bugger's ga'en tae eat it a'" came clearly through the open window. Adult faces reddened with embarrassment, and the minister's hand stopped in mid air, it hovered for a second or two before finally taking a very small second portion, which I imagine had almost choked him. No doubt there were a few skelpit erses in the hoose that nicht.

Teddy, as I said earlier was a casualty of the war, although he saw no fighting. Having been in the Territorials, he had been keen to serve his country, but because of his injuries during training, he eventually left the Gordon Highlanders after months in hospital and found work in Civvy Street. His first marriage broke up, as did that of many others, probably due to the pressures of the war and separation. The Government at the time, recognising the difficulties many couples were having in staying together, brought in quick and easy divorces. On top of his injuries Teddy little needed this extra stress.

Later he married again and settled down in Stonehaven. He and I were for some reason, always quite distant, maybe because there was 15 years age difference between us, but I remember him best for his very keen sense of humour. He was always ready with a witty reply to any remark. "Aye, Teddy can aye mak ye lauch", Mum would say. The only times I saw Teddy lose his rag were when he had to work wi Tam. Bit of coorse thon horse wid've tried the patience o' a saint, as the saying goes. I liked the atmosphere in our house when Teddy or Alfie was around. Mum was always in a good mood when any of her loons was visiting.

Sandy eventually got home from the Far East, and within a few months was demobbed. All the servicemen were given a complete set of new clothes on demob, including a suit. Sandy told us that, when he went to be kitted out with his new clothes, he said "I telt them far tae stick their suit". He was pretty disillusioned when he saw the demob clothes. He considered them to be cheap and shoddy looking. After the years spent serving their country he felt that all the servicemen deserved better. Sandy came home a totally changed, somewhat bitter person. Barely more than a child at seventeen when he joined up, full of patriotism, an wintin tae dae his bit like abody else, he returned mentally and emotionally scarred with the sights he witnessed and experiences he lived through in the war against Japan. There was no counselling or support of any kind, and a neighbour's son whose war service was identical to Sandy's although they never actually met up, spent years in a mental hospital after his demob.

We considered we were lucky to have Sandy home with us again and putting his life back together. The years in the lives of most servicemen when they would have been training and building up skills, had been given to their country, and after the war unskilled low paid jobs were what many of them had to settle for. This was so for Sandy. The practical joker side of him had gone forever, but his kind gentle side, especially to me, eventually returned, and he met his Cathie soon after the war and within a few months they too were married. Now I had another sister in law and my world was widening. I spent a lot of time with Sandy's Cathie as they lived quite near. The two Cathies, and Violet too, were good for me.

Around this time Gladys left the family home, and with help from Alfie and Teddy found somewhere to live. Just before this happened I had discovered that Gladys wasn't what, at that time, I called my real sister. She had been born illegitimate, a great shame at that time, and taken into the family when a few days old. Today childless couples pay vast sums of money to get a baby, but at that time it was common practice for unwanted children to be advertised, and the birth mother would pay a sum of money to the prospective parents to cover some of the cost of rearing the child. In some respects it was a business arrangement, with the child sometimes finding a place in the affections of the family, but sadly this didn't always happen. In the case of Gladys it was difficult to tell. I know Teddy and

Alfie cared for her, but she and Sandy were always quite distant. Mum and Gladys certainly didn't get on well together, and she and I had always fought. I was resentful of her a lot of the time and she of me, but yet I was still upset and strangely uneasy when she left. I admired the way she accepted her situation, although she was deeply distressed about having to leave the family home. I now enjoyed having a bedroom of my own, but I didn't get any more clothes than before. What clothes I did get though no longer came from the second hand shops in Aberdeen. Perhaps it was unfair of me to blame this on Gladys, but that was how I perceived it at the time. The embarrassment of going out wearing outdated second hand clothes was now over. It was to be months though before I understood why I felt so uneasy about Gladys' situation.

Chapter Seventeen
My world collapses.

After Gladys left and for some months I found the atmosphere at home very difficult to live with. Relations were strained between some of my brothers and my parents. It seemed to me that our family had fallen apart and would never be the same again. With vague hints and remarks from my mother, I was now worrying about all the things that had been said to me over the years, about my bad blood and coming to a bad end. I was growing up and realising that things weren't always what they appeared. There were children at school who didn't have what I regarded as a proper family. The same secrecy seemed to surround them as I felt surrounded me. Slowly and unwillingly I began to wonder if I could possibly also not be one of the family, yet my name was definitely Smith. I didn't dare ask my mother about these thoughts that I harboured. I often didn't ask her things because I knew it would be a waste of time, for she didn't usually discuss anything like that. I never even knew why Gladys had to leave the family home. With regard to my worrying thoughts, there was another reason why I didn't dare ask questions, I was too frightened to face what might be the answer. So instead, for the next few months I tiptoed around in the house trying to stay in Mum's good books and doing all that was expected of me on the croft.

One day I found my answer in the least expected way. In my bedroom there was an old wooden kist. It had drawers at one end on the inside. While I shared with Gladys this was where I kept all my clothes because she liked to have the other furniture for herself. I had no problem with this because she was older than me and needed more space. I never imagined it was any easier for Gladys to share with me, than for me to share with her. Now though I could empty the last of my things from this kist. Removing one of the drawers I noticed a piece of paper wedged behind it, and I carefully fished it out and unfolded it. It was a letter from a firm of Aberdeen lawyers to my parents and headed, "Ritchie v. Stevenson", Adoption of Beatrice Ritchie.

My full name was Beatrice Ritchie Smith and in that instant my world collapsed around me. My vague feelings of unease were confirmed and my worst nightmare had arrived. My Dad wasn't my Dad and my brothers weren't my brothers. Whose was I? At that moment it was desperately important for me to feel that I belonged to someone and that I had come from somewhere.

After the initial shock I made my way downstairs sobbing painfully. I confronted my Mum and Dad who were both in the kitchen. They were very angry with me, and Dad grabbed the letter and threw it on the fire. "That's pit an end tae that", he said. Mum shouted at me "Ye shouldna hae been rakin, fit dis it maitter?" There was no explanation and no kind reassuring word.

Over the next few weeks I was able to find out from my mother when she was in a kinder mood that the film star lady who had taken me out, was my natural mother. At least I had something to cling to, but no word was ever spoken of my father. Perhaps the Smiths knew nothing of him. Violet eventually told me that I too had been advertised, along with a very much larger sum of money than had been the case with Gladys. I at least had been adopted which poor Gladys had never been. My parents never disclosed that my adoption had been a financial transaction.

Today when everything is so different with couples desperate for children, and one parent families being so normal, it is impossible to understand how things were in the thirties and forties. There was such a stigma to being born illegitimate. Now I understood all the remarks made over the years about my bad blood, about being different and the belief that I would come to a bad end, what a legacy for any child to inherit and how deeply it hurt. I even remembered when I started school at four, overhearing the word "bastard" in relation to myself, but I was too young to know what the word meant then. I fully understood it now.

I heard Mum whispering to my brothers and other family members, "Bett kens aboot her mither". Only one person ever mentioned the subject to me and that was my brother Alfie. He assured me that I was and always would be his sister, no matter the circumstances of my birth. I clung desperately to that and was so grateful for his and his Cathie's kindness at that time, Violet too was very supportive.

With hindsight, (it's a wonderful thing) I now believe that Mum and Dad genuinely didn't see why it should matter to me, and were perhaps even hurt at my behaviour. I certainly think that my other brothers didn't speak of the subject from sheer awkwardness. How could they know how much their support would have meant to me?

After this, Mum's behaviour became more irrational, and I am now certain that she was going through a very difficult menopause with severe mental problems. What a hell that must have been for her, and having to deal with a difficult hysterical teenager as well was probably all too much for her. My longing to know more about my birth mother may have appeared to her as if I was rejecting the family who had given me a home. I still believe that all children have a right to know their circumstances of birth and thankfully my experience couldn't happen today.

With the natural resilience of youth, and knowing that at last my skeletons had all tumbled out of my cupboard, I picked myself up and got on with my life. If Dad had been prepared to discuss it, he would have said something like "Mak the best o't quine".

Chapter Eighteen
Watter inside an oot.

Life was getting back to normal following the end of the war and it was easier to get building jobs done and Mum decided she wanted a scullery. This she had never had. It was to be built on to the front of the house and we were to have a sink and a tap with water piped in from the spring just down the yard. We had no hope of hot water, but to turn on a tap instead of fetching the water in a bucket, would be very welcome. We were also going to have a Calor gas cooker and a Calor gas iron. My, we were going up in the world. Now Dad wid tackle onything given the chance, but he decided that biggin kitchens wi windaes an plumbin work wis a bit beyond im, so tradesmen were employed and we duly ended up wi oor new scullery. Mum was so proud of it. It had three large windows and she immediately set about making net curtains for them all. To finish these off she made a frilly pelmet which went from one window to the next all the way round. The new cooker sat in a corner all shiny an bright (tae start wi onywey). It was Mum's first cooker as she had only ever been used tae different ranges, or even cooking on open fires until then.

With a new clootie rug on top of the linoleum, she wis all set tae haul any unsuspecting passerby aff the road tae see her new kitchen wi runnin watter. They probably wouldn't have been all that unwilling for there was a natural nosiness amongst the fermin community. Ye did hae tae watch though that ye didna cause a speik by gettin a bittie above yersel. Ye aye hid tae ken yer place an have a very good reason for gettin onything new. In this scullery Mum was particularly proud of the net curtains she hid made on her very old treadle sewing machine. I was desperate to use this family heirloom, but my feet on the treadle jist widnae work wi ma brain, so I had to stick tae shewin athing by han.

A very few days after the kitchen was on show to willing and not so willing viewers, I put on the kettle for a cup of tea, the gas ring had to be lit with a match and we had already got into the habit of tossing the spent matches into a dish on the window ledge. This day my match was still lit when I tossed it away. The first net curtain went up in flames that travelled along the pelmet to the next one, and so on until all six curtains and the pretty frilly pelmet Mum was so proud of, were reduced to piles of ash along each of the window ledges. I stood rooted to the spot with fear until Mum appeared a few minutes later. She demanded to know fit hid happened tae her bonny screens, and I could only point shakily tae the ash on the ledges. I had got quite a fright and I think she knew that, for little was said, but there were nae mair frilly curtains beside the gas cooker to show off.

I had an experience too with the gas iron. I was scared of it from the start, as I didn't like seeing the flame burning away inside it. Inevitably something flimsy I was ironing caught fire. It happened to be something I had borrowed, so I felt very guilty about it. Just after that incident we heard from the postie that a neighbour who still had a petrol iron had left it on and had forgotton about it. It was said to have overheated, exploded and gone through the ceiling into the bedroom above. We had got rid of our petrol iron when we got the gas one, but I wasn't too sure that we hadn't got out of the frying pan and into the fire.

Fire was always a worry to farmers because of the lack of water at hand. We were lucky to have our spring so near and we had the dam that was almost always full. Of course the croft wouldn't have been built where it was without these reliable sources of water. Our spring supplied the house and had never been known to dry up even in the hottest summers.

The drinking water for the animals came from either the dam, that filled the old bath (the one Teddy went headfirst into thanks to Tam) or one of the many little burns and ditches running alongside the fields. These filled conveniently placed drinking troughs for the animals, usually old sinks. One previous very dry summer when Gladys was still living at home, Dad decided that just in case of a water emergency, we would all go out into the fields and dowse for a back up spring. Now, although this may seem odd to some of you, it was a very natural thing for us to do. None of us were dowsers except Dad, who had had a shottie at it in his younger day he said, but fit did that maitter, we could dae onything if we tried or so he always telt us. He cut forked hazel twigs for the four of us. Hazel was said to be best because the trees grow naturally near or sometimes in water and for this reason it was believed they were the most suitable for finding it.

Dad showed us how to hold our dowsers lightly in our hands, and told us what to expect. Slowly we paced the fields and suddenly Gladys' twig started to vibrate wildly until she couldn't hold it – but nor did she want to. Having no belief in this dowsing business whatsoever, she was terrified to find it actually worked. She screamed, threw her dowser into the air and made for the house in terror. Nothing would tempt her to have any more to do with that spooky business she said.

Mum and I were very comfortable with dowsing that day and didn't find it the least bit spooky, and we now knew where to find water if the need arose. We didn't know how far down we would have to dig but at least we knew it was there. It was all a good education for me when I came to teach dowsing many years on, and I still dowse today, although with slightly more sophisticated brass rods for outdoors and pendulums for indoors.

Chapter Nineteen
Fae horse tae tractor

One unforgettable day came when Dad announced that Tam wis jist fair past it an he wid hae tae go. We wir gettin a tractor, an this wid be anither steppie up in the fermin world for us. I am thoroughly ashamed to admit that I shed not a single tear for Tam. I was vaguely troubled about the tinned dog food thing, so I was very careful not to ask if that would be Tam's fate. Where he went and what happened to him was never mentioned. In order to justify, to some extent, getting rid of him, Dad said that at least tractors didn't eat when they weren't working. Unlike the rest of us though, he was greatly put out to see Tam go. He felt that he had served us well and of course, having worked with horses all his cottaring days, Dad was going to have to be the auld dog that wid hae tae learn new tricks.

Getting a tractor that was very old and had four iron wheels wasn't of great interest to me. You see I knew nothing about tractors, certainly couldn't, and indeed I was far too young to drive, so why would I be concerned about a tractor? Oh what a fool I was. I never stopped to think that I had been scared of horses, knew less than nothing about them, but still ended up as second horseman. But never for one moment did I think I would be expected tae drive a tractor. Now what I didn't know was that Dad hid niver driven a tractor either. He wis gey clever tae keep that under his bonnet. I only realised that recently when my brother Alfie and I were comparing notes. I also discovered that Dad never mastered reversing the tractor when the trailer was attached. Alfie would be asked up at a weekend sometimes "tae gie's a hand" as Dad put it, but really this was to catch up with any of the reversing jobs that needed doing. A master of deceit wis my Dad, an there wis me believin he could dae onything.
Many a happy hour Dad hid pickin up fit he needed for this tractor, second hand of course, or maybe even fourth or fifth. Bein a gie auld machine it hid tae be matched up wi gie auld implements, although lack of money would have had more to do with that than anything. I suspect half the fun o' gettin this

tractor for Dad wis in ha'en an excuse tae ging tae a roup if it wis at the weekend, an the mart when there wis an unction on.

Dad got fair cairried awa at ony o' the sales. The unctioneers of the time were real comedians and it wis a wonderful afternoon's entertainment jist tae stan an listen tae them. Unfortunately Dad could niver resist bidding. (A habit he smit me wi, an I still hiv tae bide awa fae roups.)

On one occasion he happened to be at the mart wi a man he worked wi. Adam wis badly needin a lawnmower, so fin ane cam up at the sale Dad bid forrit an got it for next tae nothin. Adam lived in the miller's house at Dunbar's meal mill where Dad now worked and so on the Monday morning the two of them wid try this mower out on Adam's overgrown lawn. It was completely useless and definitely not repairable.

Nothing daunted and tae mak the best o' a bad deal, the two of them sandpapered it all down, painted it bright green with touches of yellow, and entered it for the next sale in a fortnight's time. I gather it looked very good and they were quite confident they would get their money back with a bittie profit. Neither of them had any conscience whatsoever. Jist the opposite in fact – they were fair prood o' themselves an it wid be a good story tae tell.

Come the next sale, this tarted up heap of junk sold readily and a very handsome profit was made. Neither Dad nor Adam had actually been at the sale, but on the Monday they collected their ill-gotten gains and shared them.

A few days later Mum, Dad and I cried in on Alfie and Cathie at Brickfield, an Dad couldna wait tae tell them how clever he and Adam had been. He fair enjoyed regaling Alfie wi every detail. At the end of the tale, told wi much lauchin on Dad's part, a now very quiet Alfie asked us to go out to his garden shed wi im. Hiding inside wis the bright green and yellow lawnmower. Alfie had been completely taken in by it because it looked almost new, and he hid been fair lookin forrit tae tryin it oot. So who had the last laugh, certainly not Dad for of course he gave Alfie his money back and the mower couldn't go into the sale for a third time. Being painted bright green and yellow it would be readily remembered. With our family sense of humour though it was all considered worth it, for wasn't it the best laugh they'd had in a long time?

Dad did have more luck wi the implements he bought tae work wi the tractor, and I wis lookin forrit tae sittin back an watchin a this work going on, wi Dad as tractorman. Now jist how naïve wis that then?

Chapter Twenty
Gettin oot an aboot mair

With more petrol available for the car, we were able to travel a little further afield than the occasional visit to the pictures in Stoney. Of course I had been making weekly visits there on a Saturday night on my own for some time. For the work I did on the croft I earned an old shilling a week. This was enough for a seat in the ninepennies at the pictures and the remaining 3d paid my bus fare there and back. After Sandy came home to stay and before he married Cathie, he would give me a little extra for a treat. This was very generous of him considering how little he himself had.

It was in the front row of the pictures that I smoked my first (and last, as it happened) cigarette. I suppose I had taken it from Dad's Woodbine or Gold Flake packet along with a few matches. I had only taken one or two puffs trying hard to inhale, when I was violently sick. Just as well I was in the front row. I wasn't too popular with the usherette that night. I have never touched a cigarette since, nor been tempted, for even someone else's smoke still makes me feel nauseous.

The films I saw transported me to another world. Emotionally I could slip into the main female character's part with ease. I seesawed from being grief stricken to ecstatic. I was totally in love with my hero, Alan Ladd, and I took a long time to forgive Sandy for pointing out to me that this heartthrob of mine was actually very short in stature, and wore built up shoes to bring him up to the height of his co-stars.

One evening for a change, Mum, Dad and I went to a basket whist held in Cookney Hall. They both liked a hand of whist. I don't remember the fourth person that night that made up the table, but they were providing the 'basket'. This was the most common type of whist drive held around the country halls at the time. One person would "tak a table" and they didn't pay, but had to bring three other players with them who did. This person also brought, in a basket (hence the name "basket whist") supper for all the players at their table.

Now these whists were a great opportunity for the hostess to show off her baking skills tae abody. After the card playing was over it was time for supper. At each table the very best teacloth and china would be produced with a great flourish from the basket, followed by sandwiches, scones, pancakes and jam and cream sponges. There was much peeking at the other tables "tae see fit kin o'a spread so and so's pittin on". Basket whists were very popular because of this rivalry (not always friendly by any means) as because of it "ye could aye depend on a good feed", people would say.

The actual whist playing was a nightmare for me because it was all taken so seriously, and to inadvertently trumph yer pertner's trick was little short of treason, and wid be cast up at every opportunity even as much as a year later. I've noticed some card players are like elephants – they never forget. I widna be surprised if someone trumphin their pertner's trick at a whist hidna started a war somewhere in the world.

On this occasion there was a dance after the whist and Mum and Dad said we could stay for a whilie an listen to the Scottish Country Dance music. A boy asked me to dance and suddenly I was in another unexplored world – I had found boys. There was only one drawback that night – the tackets in my shoes. When I got home I pulled them all out with a pair of pliers and never let on. I wisna gaen tae be embarrassed like that again.

The next social occasion of importance in my life was a visit to see a drama production by the Cookney Amateur Dramatic Society. This too was followed by a dance. I was totally carried away by the drama bit and knew at once that this was what had been missing from my life. I would be an actress. I joined the Dramatic Society immediately and for the next few years I had a marvellous time making friends and touring the local area with our annual productions. It didn't take long for me to realise that a famous actress I would never be, but I loved every minute I was showing off. Unfortunately I never got a real drama queen role I was too young they said.

Being part of the cast meant plenty of partners for the

dances that followed. A quick kiss and a cuddle behind the hall with a boy that took my fancy was usual too – nothing more mind you. To allow a hand up your blouse earned a girl the reputation of being fast. Goodness knows what life would have been like at home for me if I had let that happen. My mother was getting more and more paranoid about me "keepin masel decent" as it wis.

One winter word got round of a dance and beauty competition to be held in Cookney Hall, when the prettiest girl would be chosen to be Cookney Queen, and her photograph would be in the Press and Journal on the Monday. I had never wanted anything so much in the whole of my life than to be Cookney Queen. I couldn't wait for that Friday night to come along. I was sure, with the conceit of youth that I would win. On the Thursday, the day before this earth trembling occasion, disaster struck. My face started to throb and swell, and by that evening I had an ugly boil on my cheek. My first step on the ladder to fame as a beauty queen was not to be.

Chapter Twenty One
Things tak a turn for the worse again.

Unfortunately back at the croft things were taking a downward turn again. It was all because of this tractor Dad had bought. I overheard Dad say to Mum "Bett'll easily drive the tractor. She's a gallus quine, she'll manage fine". I had learned early on that anytime Dad used the words gallus quine, I was gaen tae be telt I hid tae dae somethin I wisna gaen tae like.

The very thought of driving the tractor terrified me. Now that I know that Dad had never driven a tractor either, I realise that it was a case of the blind teaching the blind. To be true there wasn't a lot to learn, and Dad now had some experience driving the car. I had a bit of a problem with the steering because these old iron wheeled tractors were very heavy and it took all my strength to pull the wheel round on the corners. However it was actually stopping the tractor that had me totally baffled. I just could not get the hang of it and perhaps there was a degree of not really wanting to.

Now I understand that with these old tractors the clutch and brake were on the same pedal, so to stop I had to put my wellie booted foot on this pedal and press down. This operated the clutch bit, but if I wanted to brake, this pedal had to be pressed further down to the floor. For the tractor to stay put but with the engine running, there was a little metal hook fixed to the floor and this had to be looped over the pedal to hold it down. It all sounds so simple and yet I was incapable of doing this, except by accident. I never seemed to press the pedal hard enough and the tractor would chug on, and by the time I realised that it wasn't going to stop, it was often too late. Fortunately some of the time it didn't matter where exactly I stopped and I usually settled for anything within five to ten yards of where I wanted to be. However all the fields around the croft were bordered by drystone dykes and before we got the tractor they were in quite a good state of repair. I quickly learned that a drystane dyke hid nae chance when attacked by an iron wheeled tractor wi me at the wheel. It usually gave in quite quickly. We soon had a succession o' gaps in oor dykes. These were rebuilt at intervals by Dad who claimed he had done a bit o' dykin in his younger day and why should I doubt him, he hid done a'thing else it seemed.

Dad demolished the dyke himsel though ae time, an it wis richt next tae the road tae. I secretly enjoyed this, until I overhead him tell Mum later in the week, that a neighbour had stopped in the passin for a crack an hid mentioned the dyke. This neighbour apparently said "Wullie, your lassie his a richt ill will at dykes". Dad told Mum "Ah niver let on it wis me, ach he'll be nane the wiser". Dad could be a richt traitor fin he liked.

I got on really well with the tractor when I was harrowing. I could catch any missed bits the next time round and it didn't matter if I covered some ground twice. Unfortunately at some point I had been elevated to second tractorman for ploughing. This was a huge responsibility for one so young and a quine at that and I never quite knew how it came about. Dad said ploughing was easy. All I had to do was fix my eyes on a spot at the end of the field and "Mak straight forrit" he said. There was the added complication of having to turn round every few yards to check that I still had the plough behind me. Ours was quite stony ground and although the plough could push small stones aside, if it hit a big one it would simply detach itself from the tractor. Of course this was a safety feature but it happened all the time and it was very time consuming having to reverse and hitch the plough back on to the tractor.

One day I was ploughing in a field next the main road and my brother Sandy was on the plough. I was trying hard to keep my dreels straight and check that I still had the plough attached, when, on the road ahead, I could see two young lads who seemed quite interested in me, well they kept waving to me anyway. I was going to a dance at Cookney that night and my mind turned to wondering if they might be going too, and which one did I fancy. I was conceited enough to think I had the choice. Well, as you can guess I forgot about my stopping distance and headed the tractor through the dyke yet again, richt aside them. If that wasn't bad enough I then found out they hadn't been waving *to* me, they had been waving *at* me and they were jist tryin to tell me that I hid left Sandy an the ploo back at the ither end o' the field. That dented my pride for a whilie, an I wis richt gled they werena at the dancin that nicht efter a.

One winter morning we woke to deep snow, and Dad started work quite early. As often happened with cars at that time, because of the extreme cold, the auld Fordie wouldn't start. Mum came upstairs to wake me and tell me to get some clothes on as Dad needed a tow wi the tractor. Of course it was quite illegal to drive an iron wheeled tractor on a public road for obvious reasons. We did it just the same when we wanted to go from one field to another, and we would drive with two wheels on the verge and two on the road.

This day I wis richt sweirt tae get oot o' ma bed an inta ma cauld wellies tae drive the tractor, bit Dad hid tae get tae work. By the time I appeared outside Dad had the tractor started up and out of its wooden shed. He had no problem reversing without the trailer, and the car and tractor were all fixed up with a tow rope between them. All I had to do I was told, was to drive slowly up the side road, and with any luck the car would start afore I reached the main Netherley to Stonehaven road. My luck was out and it didn't, so I had to make my way gingerly down the main road half on the verge, until the engine of the car eventually gave a splutter and reluctantly sprang to life. In an instant Dad was out of the car, unhitched the rope and was off with a shout "See an pit the tractor back in the shed noo, Bett". Now how dangerous an order was that then?

First I had to get this cumbersome collection of metal turned round and over onto the other side of the road, always remembering that there was a ditch there hidden under the snow. I prayed and prayed that the engine wouldn't stall, for I would not be able to start it again. It needed a man's strength tae crank the handle at the front. I had been warned never to try as, if there was a kick back, I might be injured. There wis nae need tae worry on that score, I wisna keen on tractors an even less keen on startin them. I micht hae been a gallus quine, but I wisna a daft gallus quine.

I made it slowly back down to the yard where Mum was waiting for me and now all I had to do was get the tractor back in the shed. It was a narrow door, or so it appeared to me who had never tackled this manoeuvre before. Ducking down as I moved forward, I got the tractor halfway in, I should then have started the stopping bit, if you get my drift. Well I didn't, and the tractor and I chugged on into the end wall and halfway through before the engine stalled. I quickly scrambled off and out of the shed. Mum and I stood and watched in disbelief as the sides and roof of the shed slowly collapsed round the tractor. It all seemed to happen in slow motion. What a sorry sicht for Dad tae come hame tae that nicht an I wis richt gled he hid done a bit o' joinerin in his young day alang wi a'thing else he boasted aboot.

I realised there was no advantage to me in changing from horse to tractor and Dad persisted in making me drive and in a very few years when I was old enough, and there still being no driving test required, he was very insistent I apply for a driving licence. "Tae get ye on the road wi the car" he said with great enthusiasm. I dug my heels in on this one and refused, no doubt doing all the other road users of the time a huge favour. Na, na Stoney wisna ready for me ahint the wheel o' a car jist yet.

Chapter Twenty Two
Fae gallus quine tae Miss Smith.

Back in 1948 I was nearing the end of my schooldays and, because of the raising of the leaving age to 15 I was going to have to return to the Academy after the summer holidays until my birthday in October. As you can imagine this didn't please me one little bit, but it had to be. All that year getting a job was uppermost in my mind, but such is the influence of preconditioning, although my greatest wish was to work in a chemist's shop, it never once occurred to me that there was no real reason why I shouldn't do this. But I had been told I was to work in an office so that was the direction I looked in to find work, as my parents would have considered doing anything else a waste of my education. If they had only realised how little of that education I had actually absorbed, things might have been viewed differently. I scraped through my exams, or not, as was the case in some subjects. What else could I expect? My schoolwork always had to come second to croft work, but it is too easy to blame my lack of achievement on that. Better to face the truth. It is difficult to study and do well when you are a square peg in a round hole. Shorthand, typing and particularly bookkeeping held no appeal for me. I would so much rather have been doing something creative.

In spite of this I found a job and the Monday after breaking up for the summer holidays, I started work in a solicitors' office in Stonehaven. I was to work full time for the summer, then after going back to school, on weekdays I would go in after four o'clock and on Saturday mornings until my birthday when I would have a permanent position. I considered myself lucky and Mum and Dad were very pleased. I wis makin somethin o' masel. My full time pay was, in old money, a pound a week, it seemed like a small fortune to me, but small was always the operative word. With my social life expanding, I wis aye needin something new tae wear, an a pound didna go far. The Co-op restaurant on Evan Street had an offer of weekday lunches for ten shillings, and taking advantage of this accounted for half my salary. It does seem a bit posh tae ca a pound a week salary, bit that wis law offices for ye.

My job title was "trotter". Now just how glamorous wis that? But it was descriptive, for I trotted to the post office, the bank, and anywhere else I was sent. All town mail was hand delivered, and I quickly learned that I could save my legs by meeting up with other trotters and swopping letters. One of the advantages of my job was that I could run errands for myself or for my workmates, using the excuse, "I'm going to the Post Office to buy stamps". I really enjoyed the freedom of this, and I knew what was on display in every clothes shop window at any time, and which days the displays were changed. I think this may be called "skiving". On my very first day I was caught out by an old practical joke, common in offices at the time. I was sent to the chemist to buy a bottle of avizandum ink. I didn't stop to think why a chemist's shop would stock ink and what was avizandum ink anyway? I was pretty naïve and trusting. Now I knew how Sandy felt when people kept asking him for "hingin mince" on his first days at the butchers. Bit it wis a meant in good fun an wisna sair.

As well as all the trotting I did, I was also, amongst other duties, expected to "book" the letters before posting. This involved copying them into a huge book made up of very thin pages. The letters were placed face down in this book and covered with damp sheets of cloth. The book was then placed in an enormously heavy press. It was tightened sufficiently (quite dificult to do), to allow the print of the letters, aided by the dampness from the cloths, to be copied on to the pages of the book. A clean, legible copy was the aim, and I rarely achieved either. Maybe this was because the water to dampen the cloths was at the top of three flights of stairs. Either my cloths were too dry because I was too lazy to climb the stairs to wet them, or they were too wet, because I overdid the water to save having to make a second journey. I well remember my excitement when we had our very first visit from a rep selling a new discovery –

carbonpaper. Fit a godsend that wis tae me, an nae doot tae abody else that hid tae read my copied letters.

Solicitors' offices were very formal and the work mostly deadly dull. I was always Miss Smith even to my work colleagues. I shared the front office with two others, one an older lady who was the cashier, and when I got to know her I found she was good fun, and she covered up my shortcomings quite often. I was immensely grateful to her for this and particularly on one occasion. The senior partner always came to the office dressed in a black suit, white shirt with a wing collar and black bowler hat. He wasn't known for his extravagances when it came to buying new clothes. Come tae think o't he wisna kint for his extravagances fin it cam tae onythin. On arrival each day, his bowler hat would be placed on top of a heavy safe, which stood just inside the door and in front of the very high window in our office. This hat had, over the many years of its life, some said since he was an apprentice law clerk even, faded to a peculiar dark green colour in places. On the inside, it showed the stains of Brylcreme to a disgusting degree. We all took bets on how much longer it would last without falling apart. One day to the astonishment of all, our boss appeared in a new bowler hat. After he had gone upstairs to his own office we all examined it closely, hazarded guesses about the cost and carefully put it back on the safe in front of the window exactly as we had found it.

Later that day, it being hot and sunny, I was instructed to open this window. To do so I had to use a very long heavy pole and it was always a tricky operation. This day the window appeared to have stuck and I had to exert a lot of force before it finally gave in and slid down with a soft plop. Only then did I look down to find that the end of the pole had been resting on the new bowler, and this now had a very neat round hole on the top and it was skewered on the end of the pole. I didn't know whether to laugh or cry but settled on laughing along with the others in the room.

The kindly cashier came to my rescue and carefully pushed the flap back into place, fortunately a scrap had stayed attached like a little hinge. She smoothed down the felt carefully and finally brushed up the pile with a little clothes brush she kept in her desk. The repair wasn't too noticeable. That evening, to my great relief, the bowler sailed off home on the head of its unsuspecting owner without comment. He hidna noticed! A few days later he appeared wearing another new bowler, but from that day on this one went upstairs to his own office and remained in a place where he could keep a close eye on it. We all wondered with great enjoyment, what explanation he had come up with to explain how such a neat round hole could have appeared in his brand new hat.

I climbed the ladder in that office from trotter to shorthand typist. My shorthand skills were only a little better than my driving, but I muddled through. A lot of the dictation was routine stuff that I could have done on my own and when stuck, I would scribble the odd difficult word in longhand. I knew I wasn't going to rise to any dizzy heights in the office world, but fit did that maitter, and at least my typing was good and practical jokes too were a specialty of mine and usually appreciated by the other members of staff.

I narrowly missed being sacked on one occasion. I was working for the senior partner by this time (nae mair jaunts tae the post office for me) and his education had gaps in it (as if I wis een to speik). He had worked up from law clerk to solicitor without going to university. One day I queried a word in his dictation and he abruptly replied that I wasn't paid to think, I was paid to do what I was told. On the following day he dictated another letter to a big law firm in Aberdeen and in it he apologised for a previous "typ-ical" error. Of course he meant "typographical" error, but without the hyphen it read as "typical" error, and a mistake like this wasn't going to do our reputation any good as a law firm. Well, still smarting from the put down of the day before, I let the irresponsible side of me rule my head. I also knew that the previous error was his and not mine, so I typed the letter as dictated. After enduring a huge dressing down later from the other partner when the copy letters were checked for charging to the clients, I smiled sweetly and repeated to him what I had been told about not being paid to think. Efter that incident there wis a bit o' frost hinging aboot in the air for a whilie and if it had been today, I would have been on a warning.

This incident led me to move to another post in Aberdeen in a similar but much bigger office. Although I had a longer day because of the bus timetables, I enjoyed the travelling. There was always something to see or find amusement in. For instance, one very rainy day my attention was drawn to the rain hat of the lady sitting in front of me. On top of her felt hat she was wearing a pair of baby's plastic pants with the holes for the legs closed up with safety pins. Smiling at things like that was a good way to start my day, an it wis a good story tae tak hame at nicht.

In the new office I was quite excited to be working at a desk overlooking busy Union Street, and I had all those clothes shops and chemists to browse in during my lunch hour. What more could a country lassie ask for? One particularly hot week I had dressed for work each day in a nice skirt and fresh short sleeved blouses looking quite smart and thinking that, just maybe, I was an upwardly mobile secretary after all. Towards the end of that week, I was told our office manager wanted to speak with me. Had she discovered my shorthand weakness? I was a wee bit apprehensive but she greeted me kindly and came straight to the point. She said "Miss Smith, the senior partners have asked me to tell you that they would like you to wear long sleeved blouses in the office in future". Then, lowering her voice, she whispered, "You see the sight of your bare arms is overexciting the male members of staff". Jist as weel they didna ken I had aince flashed my knickers at a passin stranger – even though I wis only three.

After a few months I came to realise that I didn't really fit into a big office and the city lights were dimming a little for me. With so little money to spend the shops had lost much of their attraction and when my old boss appeared one evening holding an olive branch and offering me my old job back with more money, I was happy to return to my beloved Stoney.

I did miss my comfortable bus rides to and from work. The bus times to Stoney didn't fit my office hours and I had given up on my bicycle. It was difficult to find some place to leave it during the day. My bike had been stolen on one occasion and I had been reluctant to report this, because if the police had found it they would certainly have charged me with something, for I never had working brakes or a rear reflector. Rarely did I have lights, or if I had, the batteries were likely to be flat. You can see why I didn't want any police involvement. I was surprised that my bike had been stolen at all. The thief obviously hadn't looked at it closely, or else they wir aff their heid.

I did have frequent lifts to work though. Nae fairmer wid pass Fishermyre's lassie walkin in the road withoot stoppin. If they hid their car that day so much the better, bit if it wis a tractor day I wid even be gled o'a lift on the back o' their trailer. At times I would arrive at the office speckled with mud from hair to shoes. This mud would fly off the tractor wheels as we bowled along. On occasions there was worse. If the farmer had been using the tractor to spread dung on the fields I would be liberally sprayed wi sharn, an I wid sneak up the three flights o' stairs tae clean masel up an hope naebody could smell me in the meantime.

Those were such trusting times to live in. A passing stranger only had to stop and tell me he knew my father and it would have been considered perfectly safe for me to accept a lift from him. Vehicles rarely passed any walker without offering a lift. I occasionally travelled in the school taxi when there was a vacant seat, but someone reported the taxi owner and he had to reluctantly pass me on the road after that, or risk losing the school contract. Some time on I repaid his kindness in a small way by hiring his taxis for my wedding day.

My most unusual form of transport to the office was a Bren gun carrier. A young man who lived further up Netherley had bought it after the war, and when passing he always stopped to offer me a lift. Bren gun carriers aren't easy things to climb into wearing a tight skirt, but with help I made it. It was a noisy, very bumpy ride. Because of its caterpillar tracks it bounced down the road making me feel ever so slightly nauseous. Not to attract attention I was always dropped off before the town centre. I seem to remember there was a slight problem over whether passengers were covered by insurance or not, so it was best I wasn't seen. I enjoyed these lifts immensely. Not many of my friends could say they travelled to the office in a Bren gun carrier. Perhaps not many of my friends would have wanted to. Sadly these lifts came to an abrupt halt. One icy snowy day, and I wasn't a passenger at the time, the carrier skidded turning from Allardyce Street into Evan Street and partly demolished the front of the newsagents'shop on the corner. It wis back tae Shanks pony for me, an there wisna a lot comin ower me wi that.

Chapter Twenty Three
Yefurup?

At the time of starting work and having found this new interest – boys – I set my sights on going to the dancing in the Town Hall in Stonehaven. My friend Marjorie and I had tried a couple of weeks at the Alexandria in Cameron Street where most of the young country folk went, but neither of us had any great hankering after being farmers' wives. Marjorie knew nothing of country living and I knew too much. Of course it must be realised that at that time girls were always on the lookout for a suitable, very handsome, very rich boy to marry and young though we were, Marjorie and I were no exception. We decided to try pastures new and the Town Hall had the added advantage of being where all the summer visitors gathered.

Stonehaven was a very busy seaside holiday resort with a few hotels and many boarding houses. Visitors were mostly from Glasgow with some from Edinburgh. The Council put a great deal of effort into providing entertainment and employed a "big" band for the summer months, and for quite a few years this was the Harry Margolis Band. Appointed also by the Council was an official photographer. The members of the band and the photographer worked hard with very long hours. In the afternoons the Band provided entertainment at the heated outdoor pool, and often after they had finished at the Town Hall in the evening, there was midnight bathing at the pool with more music.

Every Saturday during the holiday months, a fresh influx of visitors would arrive in the town, providing us young ones with new "talent" as we called them. Rarely did any of them stretch to staying two weeks, unless they were camping or staying in a caravan. To us girls anyone who could spend even a week in a boarding house or hotel had to be well off. Up to that time I had never been on a train, and had only slept away from home once when I went to stay with Violet and Wullie in Gourdon. I was about five at the time and I pee'd the bed with excitement, or fear. I don't remember which, but I do know I've never done it again and I was never asked back. Can you blame them?

Summers were wonderful in Stonehaven around this time. If a girl was in a relationship with a local boy when the visitors started arriving, this would be broken off until the autumn so that they could both play the field. Any couple staying together during the summer was destined for engagement, marriage, sex, somewhere to live and kids in that order. Girls would fall head over heels in love on the Saturday night with a visitor, always the opposite sex, say cheerio to him on the following Friday promising to write daily and be true forever, but start again with someone else the next night. With any luck this could go on for the whole summer. After that it was back to the local talent.

Every Saturday night Marjorie and I filed into the town hall. After leaving our coats in the cloakroom we moved towards the inside door of the hall. We might of course have applied yet another coat of lipstick to the already overdone mouth and yet another fluff of powder to the cheeks. We handed over our entrance money and had the inside of one of our wrists stamped to prove that we had paid. If the stamp was damp we might dash out and transfer it to a friend's wrist. Nowadays that would be called a twofor, i.e. two for the price of one. Marjorie and I were a bit wimpish about doing that and only risked it if funds were very limited.

For us the members of the band were wonderful and a date with one of them was our dream. It never happened. Probably they were all so tired after a day's work that they went straight back to their digs and fell into bed. Girls didn't do beds with boys at that time. The most daring thing allowed was a hand inside a blouse behind the swimming pool wall. And that was only if they were "serious" and likely to get engaged. Of course, *I* didn't do that either! I had to be especially careful where boys were concerned because of my background. When I learned of my adoption I understood the meaning of the words "bad blood will oot" and "come tae a bad end". In my naivety when I was small, I had always imagined this to have something to do with my death. I had surmised this might come sooner rather than later, so it was quite a relief in a way to discover that as long as I "kept masel decent" I would be in no danger of "gingin the wye o' ma mither". Now I can laugh about it all but these were genuine fears Mum had for me and isn't it sad to think that these beliefs about illegitimate baby girls were still so prevalent.

Back to the Town Hall, the girls sat down the right hand side of the dance floor with the boys opposite. Except for the "ladies excuse me" the boys had to make the approach. Now, we girls could tell a lot from how this was done. Some would come straight over and jerk their head silently towards the dance floor. I turned them down making some silly excuse for not dancing. I liked to be asked properly. Of course, I would then have to dash out to the loo and apply even more lipstick and powder just to save hurting the boy's feelings. There was an unwritten rule that if a girl turned down one boy she couldn't then accept an invitation for that dance from anyone else. Another approach would be a "Ye dancin' or yefurup"? He had a 50/50 chance of acceptance depending on whether he was a smasher or not. A smasher was a rather good-looking boy or girl. Then we might have the polite "Would you like to dance this one?" Now that was my kind of partner. There was also the show off, who bowed with a flourish, extended an arm and said something like "May I have the pleasure?" He had to be watched. His was the hand that might slip down over your bum if they dimmed the lights, and that was not allowed because that would get a girl the reputation of being "fast".

We waltzed, foxtrotted and quickstepped our way through the evening. By the interval (the band needed a twenty minute break) we girls would all have hoped to be booked for the last waltz. This was important because it was the lead in to asking to see you home. To be seen home by someone meant we had "clicked", the whole object of the evening. If you went to the dances you were available for dating. When a couple became an item, they would start going to the pictures, where they could smooch in the darkness of the back row. I can still experience the atmosphere of excitement during the last waltz. The lights were dimmed, the band played very slowly, our heads touched our partner's cheek, usually damp with perspiration, bit fit did that maitter, and we shivered with anticipation of what might yet be to come. I had a slight problem when it came to the "seeing you home" bit of the evening. Since the summer visitors were mostly toonsers none fancied a six-mile round trip tae see me hame, I wisna that much o' a catch, so to get to the dances, I would risk taking my bike. I usually left it hidden somewhere around the meal mill where Dad worked. I was never left sitting out the last waltz, a huge embarrassment tae ony lassie, but instead of a request to see me home, a boy would ask "Can a see ye tae yer bike?"

At the end of that wonderful summer which, for me, seemed to last forever, when I was still only fifteen, during the last waltz a local boy asked to see me home – and he meant *home*. Within a few weeks we were going to the pictures and Marjorie was left to go dancing all on her own.

Chapter Twenty Four
Ma courtin days are here.

Frank was tall, dark and very handsome. Because of being in the Air Force he was well travelled and he was clever. This was in contrast to me, who when I met him, had only travelled a little further north of Aberdeen and as far south as Montrose. He was a linotype operator with David Waldie in Stonehaven. I knew immediately that this would be no mad fling for a week. I was seriously in love and going on sixteen. I was in yet another new world and I couldn't wait to explore it.

After a suitable period I found the courage to ask Frank home to meet Mum and Dad. This was extremly brave of me because every time Mum heard that I had been seen walking with or even speaking to a boy, she would remind me of my bad blood and the dangers of this. Did every illegitimate girl child of that time carry this cross I wondered? To be fair to my Mum, I think she had been too old when I was adopted, and she had after all already brought up four boys of her own and Gladys through times of great hardship. She told me from time to time that she regretted taking me in. I'm sure this was more because of her age than for any other reason, but it hurt deeply to be told this.

But that's enough of the "poor me" stuff, all that was about to change. With great courage and much trepidation I took Frank home. The three of them liked each other immediately. Mum told me I was very lucky to have Frank and I agreed with her completely. Things got much easier at home and I started to see another side to Mum. She was always very generous to everyone else, but now this was extended to me too. Maybe in her eyes, because I was working in a law office, was now secretary to the senior partner, and had got a very nice boyfriend, I had at last made somethin o' masel.

Soon though I was faced with a life changing decision as, before I met Frank he had applied for the Australian government's £10 assisted fare and offer of a new career in that country. We knew one or two people who had done this, and indeed my friend Marjorie and her family were about to leave Stonehaven, having taken advantage of this scheme. Frank's acceptance came through and suddenly he was given a sailing date. He immediately asked if I would join him in Australia six months later, having already taken for granted that I would. Strange though it seems now, I didn't even think about my decision. Much as I loved Frank I knew deep down that my future was not in Australia, and I immediately said so. This was a huge shock to him and he couldn't understand why I hadn't spoken of this sooner. I could only reply that he had never asked. Then came what must be one of the biggest compliments I have ever had, he said "Then I'm not going either". The passage and job were cancelled and I never knew whether he regretted this decision. Somehow I don't think he did.

Six weeks past my seventeenth birthday Frank wanted us to announce our engagement I had been proposed to properly by this time and one never to be forgotten evening, he came to Fishermyre to ask Dad for his permission for us to marry. I couldna begin tae imagine fit my Dad wis gaen tae mak o' this, nae the gettin mairried bit, but the askin his permission. He wid niver hae heard o' sic a thing. The last bus back to Stonehaven passed the end of our road at ten past eleven and after a nervewracking few hours when Frank just could not bring himself to utter the words, at eleven o'clock he finally blurted out the request. Dad was, as I thought, totally astonished, but managed to come out with "Michty aye, Goad we wir beginnin tae think we'd niver get her aff oor hands". We all burst out laughing and the tension vanished. Frank then sprinted up the road for the now approaching bus. The driver fortunately saw him coming, stopped and waited for him to jump on. It might be thought that this kindness had something to do with Frank's father being his boss, but not at all, all country bus drivers were very kind and considerate. When Frank offered the penny ha'penny bus fare to the conductress, she said "Ah've coonted ma money, gie's a fag an we'll ca it quits, but for Goad's sake dinna tell yer father".

Soon after our engagement Frank took a job with the

Daily Mail in Edinburgh and I started to prepare for our
wedding. I honestly believe this was a very happy time in
Mum's life. All her laddies had wartime weddings and she just
revelled in the preparations for mine. Although money was
always scarce there was no question but that it would be found.
Getting a good deal for everything that was needed became like
a game to us and we all thoroughly enjoyed it, particularly my
Dad. It was decided that to pay for my wedding, we needed a
big litter of pigs to be ready for the mart by the end of that
September. The wedding was the beginning of October. This
was one time I willingly did more than my share of piglet sitting
with Dad. I arrived at the office in the mornings all bleary eyed
from lack of sleep. Bit fit did that maitter, I wis gettin mairried.

My evenings now changed again. I didna wint ony
clootie rugs for my bottom drawer but I embroidered linen for
myself and knitted socks galore for Frank. Although I still
couldn't master the treadle sewing machine, I made clothes for
myself all stitched by hand. A relative in Aberdeen knew a
dressmaker who made my wedding dress for two pounds. Even
at that time I couldna hae got a better deal than that. We were
still in old money of course. I borrowed a veil and this was what
caught fire from the gas iron that I told you about.

The best room was set aside for wedding presents as was
the custom, and nobody got past the croft without being dragged
in by my mother, to admire the display and given a drink.
Whisky was offered to the men and sherry or port to the ladies.
No woman would have been seen drinking whisky outside her
own house. The "hand ins" from neighbours mounted day by
day (nae winner wi my mither keepin a close eye on passers by).
"Hand ins" were small presents from anyone who didn't know
the bride or groom very well. Mum always said they were used
by fowk tae hae a nosey at fit ither fowk had gien. Perhaps there
was a little truth in this, but everyone was very generous to us
and being Fishermyre's dother would have had a lot to do with
it. My father was well liked, rogue though he was. Along with
all the other presents we were given no less than six lemonade
sets. I had never seen a lemonade set before then. I assumed

they must be something posh people used, and had no idea in what circumstances I would use one set far less six. Obviously new experiences awaited me.

Mum started buying small things for my bottom drawer from any passing tinker. Word soon got around, and every few days another one would appear with goods that Mum felt she had to buy. I had enough wooden spoons to stock a shop, butter and jam dishes to stock a tearoom and so many more small items that I have completely forgotten about. I found the welcome Mum gave these tinkers a bit over the top. Coming home from work one day there was one old lady (they all looked old to me) sitting in Dad's armchair (we wouldn't have dared). I don't know how long she had been there, but she had obviously been plied with a little too much of the whisky, port or sherry from the looks of her. When I eventually managed to get her out of the door she went stottin fae side tae side up the yard, calling back to me that she kent ah wid be blessed wi a thrang o' bairns. Would that be a blessing I wondered? My mother was so happy, generous and kind at this time and I couldn't believe she was the same person that I had rowed with for so long.

I left work a few days before my wedding day. The firm gave me five pounds as a gift. I was now earning three pounds a week, and I thought this present was very generous. The staff too gave me a gift, but on the day I left, I was a little surprised to be given another beautifully wrapped parcel from my close friends Jean Blease and Jo Dalgarno, who shared the room I worked in. This was accompanied by much giggling. Innocently I accepted this extra wedding present and by sheer good luck opened it when I was alone. I had been sharing all the present opening with Mum up until then because she so enjoyed it all.

A couple of years prior to this, the womens' weekly magazines bought and shared by the three of us had all been offering sex manuals. There were two from each magazine, six in total and if ordered, they would be sent to us in plain wrappers. Now we all felt very daring ordering anything that had to come in a plain wrapper. I took no chances though and had my copies sent c/o one of the others. On arrival we all read them from cover to cover, swopped them, talked and laughed about them, and hid them at the back of a drawer in the office where they were promptly forgotten about.

Well you can imagine what was in my beautifully wrapped parcel. I had completely forgotten that the three of us had made a pact that the first of us to get married would be the proud owner of all six books. I must have been the only bride to go on her honeymoon with six "how to" manuals. Well what else could I do? I couldn't leave them in my bedroom for my mother to find and I couldn't throw them on our rubbish heap for my Dad to find. An afore ye start winnerin', na, na wi didna need them, wi managed awfu' fine on oor ain.

A couple of days or so before the wedding I overheard murmurings from Dad of his intention to put a flag on the chimney for the big day, this was an old custom that now seems too ridiculous to contemplate. It wis like sayin "Here's an empty hoose fu o' wedding presents, jist help yersel". That was not my main worry though. I just couldn't see how my very short, well-rounded father (and that description was kind) wis goin tae get himsel on the roof tae tie a flag on oor lum, an then get himsel safely doon again. But he did and I got back to the croft after some last minute preparations in Stoney to find this huge flag flying there for a the world tae see. Well, abody roon aboot onywye. Dad always maintained that he couldna miss the chance tae let abody ken that he wis getting rid o' me at last. Believe that if you like.

The big day arrived and a very proud Dad and I got into the taxi to go to the Church. Once seated and on the way I noticed a very large spider above our heads. Now for years I had been terrified of spiders and would scream for Dad to come and remove them from my bedroom, which he did with loud mutterings that ferm quines shouldna be feart o' spiders. On pointing this one out to him in the taxi he gave a deep sigh and said "Weel quine, ye'll hae anither man noo tae get rid o' yer spiders for ye. Ah think we'll jist leave this ane be". Could it have been that he was sad to see me go?

And finally -
About my birth mother

After my marriage and move to Edinburgh it took a little time for me to get accustomed to living in the city. My couthy Mearns dialect had to go. Frank would have been the only person to understand it. So instead o' gaen up in the world I was now seriously upwardly mobile. Fit a wye o' daein.

I had to learn very quickly to stop being so trusting. Naebody in Edinburgh kint Wullie Smith, so I couldna tak ony mair lifts fae strangers. Mind you I only did it aince, so there wis nae need for a thon fuss that Frank made. I was told too that when I was asked by a handsome man on the bus to model sweaters for him, this job offer was unlikely to be what it seemed. Fit a peety, I fancied bein a model an I still think Frank gaed ower the score aboot that little episode tae. And so it went on. But I quickly learned the ways of the city and settled in working as personal assistant (a fancy title for a shorthand typist) to a peer of the realm in an office in the West End. Now at last Mum said I'd made somethin o' masel. Didn't she aye say I should work in an office?

Back at Fishermyre things were not so good. Within a few months of my leaving home Mum and Dad said they wanted to sell up. "We jist canna manage withoot ye quine, an its nae the same" said Dad. Fishermyre was sold to an American couple who also had a dream, and Mum and Dad moved into Stonehaven. I was very sad to see the croft go, and surprised and deeply touched that my parents missed me. My relationship with Mum was still really good and I knew she was now as proud of me as she was of her loons. I was content.

Frank and I bought a house in Edinburgh and our son Scott was born there. When Frank changed careers we moved to Forfar where our daughter Alison was born. From time to time I would wonder who I really was and what my birth mother was like. In spite of all I had in my life, which was so very much and I couldn't have been happier, there was always this empty space deep within me.

I was very ashamed of the fact that I didn't have a proper birth certificate. Instead I had an "Extract from the Adopted Children's Register". This piece of paper served the same purpose but I hated it and only produced it when absolutely necessary. Eventually the law was changed allowing me, and all others like me, access to our birth records. Although I wanted this so much I waited until Mum and Dad had both passed on before I applied for my proper Birth Certificate. I felt I would have been disloyal to them if I hadn't. When the copy of my Certificate arrived I can't describe my feelings. At last I felt I truly belonged somewhere and to someone. I now had my mother's full name, address at the time of my birth and place of my birth. I had never known where I was born, such a simple thing but so important. I now had a little family history. Along with the Certificate came a warning not to try to find my mother. This had to be done through a social worker. I decided against this course of action as I wasn't sure that I had the right to bring another grandparent into my children's lives, nor did I feel I had the right to intrude on my birth mother's life. I was very aware that she could have found me at any time over the years had she wished to do so. She very obviously had chosen not to. But the empty space inside me got a little bigger and what of my rights? I found too that I had been registered as "Beatrice Stevenson Ritchie". I knew Stevenson was my father's name, but it was dropped on my "Extract" bit of paper. What right had someone in an office to take from me the name my birth mother had given me and such an important link to my natural father?

The years passed and I stuck with my decision about my mother until Frank died when I was sixty-five. My son and daughter now had their own families. When I was sixty-eight I decided it could hurt no one if I were to look for someone who might have a photograph of my birth mother, and perhaps be able to tell me a little bit about her. I truly believed she was dead and I would never have embarked on the search had I thought it could possibly be otherwise. Now at last I felt the time was right for me to find out more of who I really was and why I had been adopted.

An hour spent in our local library gave me all the telephone numbers of the Ritchies in my mother's hometown. That evening on the third call I found a cousin. The following morning I had a call from another cousin who lives just fifteen miles from me and we subsequently found we even had mutual friends. She sent me photocopies of the family tree, photographs of my mother and the telephone number of an aunt. Of even more importance than that she told me my mother was still alive and living in the south of England. I was sixty-eight and she was now eighty-six and I had two half sisters. This was a lot to take in and I was given no time to do so. Events really did move far too fast for me from then on. Within a couple of days I had an invitation to an uncle's home in Aberdeen to meet my mother, who was travelling up from her home in the south to meet me. This was all to be within a week of my first phone call. Waiting for this meeting I was in turn scared, excited, emotional and numb. From the photographs I could see that she was a very beautiful woman and even just looking at these I was surprised how much love I felt for her. How could this be? I have no answer to that, I only know that it was so.

I can honestly say I was totally unprepared for what followed next. I was so looking forward to hearing how heartbroken she had been at having to part with me, how much she had missed me being part of her life and how wonderful it was to meet again. I really needed to believe that for those were my childhood dreams. I had taken with me as gifts for my mother a small album of photographs of my wedding, my children and grandchildren along with one of my embroideries. Sadly this meeting did not turn out as I expected or hoped. My mother had travelled so far and so quickly to tell me that I must stay out of her life and she asked me to promise never to make contact with my sisters. Although she did accept the embroidery she had no wish to have the photographs and barely glanced at them. Perhaps the greatest blow of all was to be told just how much my natural father's mother had paid my adoptive parents to take me away, so much for my dreams.

That is the "poor me" stuff over but I felt I had to record it. That day though I found an uncle and two aunts who are my kind of folk, we remain the greatest of friends and I am very fond of them, as I know they are of me. I am good friends too with my cousin who lives nearby and I have since met another. A fortnight or so before my seventy-fourth birthday, my uncle told one of my sisters about me. I had of course kept my promise to my mother not to contact them. The day after that birthday I welcomed to my home my sister Ann who had travelled from America and Helen from the south of England. They each had their husbands with them and, with my uncle and aunt, we lunched and spent most of that day together. I have much treasured photographs of the three of us taken on that day. Their visit had to be one of the best birthday presents I have ever had.

Our mother is still alive and is now ninety-three. My sisters tell me that I share her voice, mannerisms and love of embroidery and gardening. Of course I wish we could have some contact but I respect her wishes and her right to them. She was only eighteen and in domestic service when I was born. How must that have felt in 1933? I have no right to judge her. I believe I wis aye meant to be a crofter quine and help my Dad get his dream and I am content.

Glossary

(For those who have missed the undoubted benefit of knowing the Mearns dialect)

Ahint – behind
An foo nae? – and why not?
As ready tae row's rin – a kindly description for being a little chubby
Awa – away
Aye – always
Bairns – children
Beasties – lice
Been kame – bone comb (usually used to remove headlice)
Bide – stay
Big – build
Bloody eeseless mannie – no DIY expert
Bools – (in this context) marbles
Bothy – rough hut
Bowk – retch
Breeks – knickers
Breer – new shoots from seeds
Buddy – person
Buroo – at that time the Labour Exchange
Ca – call
Caff – chaff
Chaumer – as bothy
Cleek – hook
Cleekit – handed (as in left handed)
Clockin hen – broody hen
Coorse – wicked
Couthie – friendly
Cruik – crook
Dirl – vibrate
Dottle – small plug of tobacco left in pipe after smoking
Draw – a puff

Dreep – droplet
Eens – ones
Eeseless – useless
Erms – arms
Fa – who
Fan or fin – when
Fee – hire
Fit – what
Flech – flea
Flit – move house
Float – cart without sides
Fowk – people
Gallus – a bit daring
Garred – make (do something)
Gird – hoop
Granny sookers – peppermints
Gye – rather
Hairstin – harvesting
Hale – whole
Hoast – cough
Hud on tult – hold it carefully
Hud yer wheesht – stop talking
Hurl – a lift (as in a vehicle)
Ill-natured – bad tempered
Ingans – onions
Jeuks – ducks
Keepin on tap o't – keeping up to date (in a work situation)
Keepin oot o' langer – keeping busy so as not to get bored
Ken – know
Kist – wooden trunk
Kjarn – quite a few
Lavvie – WC
Lauch – laugh
Len o' - take advantage of (as in tak the len o')
Loons – boys
Loupit – jumped
Lugs – ears

Lum - chimney
Maill hemmer – a heavy hammer
Masel – myself
Muck oot – clean out dung
Neeps – turnips
Oxter – armpit
Pairtin – parting
Paring – peeling
Pig – an earthenware bottle for warming the bed
Pooch- pocket
Pu – pull
Quine – girl
Rag – (as in lose his rag) lose one's temper
Rakin – searching through
Ree – run (as in henrun)
Reek – smoke
Reenge – search
Richt – really
Rickle o' beens – a trifle undernourished
Rickles – piles or small heaps
Roadit – set off on a journey
Roch – rough
Roup – public auction
Sark – shirt
Saut - salt
Semmit – vest
Seuch – suck
Sharn - dung
Shaws – stalks and leaves of a plant
Shewin – sewing
Shins – ankles
Shitin - defacating
Shoogle – shake
Skelloch – wild mustard
Skelpit erses – smacked bottoms
Skirlie- a dish of onion and oatmeal cooked in lard (author's
opinion – delicious)

Skirlin – screeching
Skitter – diarrhoea
Sleekit – cunning
Sook – suck
Speik – (as in tae cause a speik) to make yourself the subject of gossip
Speirin aboot – ask around
Spleuchan – tobacco pouch
Spuggie – sparrow
Steely – a marble made of steel
Stink – a smell
Swey – an iron bar over a fire to hang a kettle or pot on
Tatties – potatoes
Telt – told
Thocht – thought (a big thocht is something needing very careful consideration)
Thrang – crowd
Thraw – wring
Thole – put up with
Tow – string
Unction – auction
Weel aff – affluent
Wi – with
Widd – wood
Wid've garred ye bowk – feel a trifle queasy
Winna – won't
Wirna- weren't
Wisnae – wasn't
Winnerin – wondering
Wye – way
Yokin - starting

Author's note – These are not the only meanings for the above words but they are the ones relevant to this story an I didna wint tae confuse ye wi ony mair.